UNLIMITED INCOME

REPLACE YOUR SALARY AND THRIVE IN RETIREMENT

IAN WYATT

WYATT INVESTMENT RESEARCH

CONTENTS

To my parents Bruce and Carol.
Thank you for your unrelenting support. You provide a
strong example that hard work, diligent savings and smart income
strategies can deliver an outstanding retirement.

CHAPTER 1

AMERICA'S BEST INCOME INVESTMENTS REVEALED

How Anyone Can Use These Simple Investments To Earn More Income, Feel Financially Secure, And Spend Their Retirement As They Please

* * *

MOST AMERICANS WANT MORE INCOME EVERY MONTH, especially as they approach retirement. It's no surprise that retirees would love to regularly receive checks that are larger and more regular than their Social Security income.

You're probably in the same situation: you want to pay your daily expenses and bills, and you want to feel safe, confident and secure in your financial situation. Not only that, but you want to spend your retirement on your own terms — and you don't want money to limit your new-found freedom.

I'm here to show you how to get started using investments in a way that's safe, predictable and straightforward to help pay for the life you want, without waiting for 30 years or more to see additional income add up in your bank account.

Imagine with me, for a moment, being in total control of your time.

Imagine that every day, you could pass the hours doing whatever your heart desires — with no time or money pressures spoiling the day for you. What would you do with your time? Would you get out on the driving range a few times a week, take long vacations to interesting parts of the world, spend more time with the family?

This is the promise of a great retirement. This is what you have to look forward to when you've chosen to wrap up your time on the clock, and when you've created a secure financial foundation for yourself. For many Americans, retirement is the time of their lives, and if you're reading this book because you want to make sure this time is as enjoyable and secure as possible, you're in the right place.

The strategies you will learn in this book are designed to add even greater potential to this new stage of your life, and will present you with all kinds of opportunities to grow your wealth — even though you're no longer working.

However, it's possible that you're here because thinking about retirement causes you a lot of anxiety. Maybe you don't have the amount of savings you thought you would by now, and you're wondering how you're ever going to make up the difference. Or maybe you had some investments that went bad and now you're worried that you won't ever get back to feeling secure about your finances. You might even feel like you *can't* retire, because you just don't have the money — even though you've been looking forward to this stage for years.

Many Americans feel this way. You're not alone, and it's not your fault.

In late 2018, the Federal Reserve published their fifth

annual report on the economic well-being of US households. While things have been improving gradually since the financial crisis of 2008-2009, we still have a long way to go for the average American to feel confident about their retirement:

Many adults feel behind in their savings for retirement. Even among those who have some savings, people commonly lack financial knowledge and are uncomfortable making investment decisions. Less than two-fifths of non-retired adults think that their retirement savings are on track, and one-fourth have no retirement savings or pension whatsoever. Three-fifths of non-retirees with self- directed retirement savings accounts, such as a 401(k) or IRA, have little or no comfort in managing their investments. On average, people answer fewer than three out of five basic financial literacy questions correctly, with lower scores among those who are less comfortable managing their retirement savings.[1]

Delving deeper into that report, I found that the average expenses for a retired couple are around $3,800 per month. Even when both people in the couple have paid into the Social Security program, their income will only be about $2,800 per month. That means that the average retired American couple earns $1,000 less than their income *every month.*

Additionally, only about 45% of American adults have a 401k retirement savings account. The average amount saved in that account is $58,000, and over half of the people with a 401k don't even have that much saved (don't forget that the 'average' takes into account all the people who have been able to max out their 401k contributions over the course of their career, so for many people, the total amount is much lower).

Even folks with $58,000 saved face challenges. For example, let's assume you take a 3% annual draw from that account. This will only provide $1,700 in annual income. That's nowhere near enough to cover the $12,000 income gap. It's clear then that while Social Security and retirement savings will take care of *some* of the needs of the average American retiree, many people are facing a huge gap in their income.

So here's what I'm hoping to accomplish with this book: I want to empower you to take control of your financial future and to show you exactly how you can bridge the gap between your expenses and your income. Assuming you've got some money saved (say, that $58,000 or so), the income investment strategies you'll discover in this book will help you to close (and maybe even surpass) that gap and ensure that your retirement is secure and comfortable for its duration.

As you read through this book, you'll discover the strategies that can help you build unlimited income — no matter where you're starting from, or what your risk tolerance is, you can use these investments to generate as much income as you need to maintain the lifestyle you want.

I want to open your mind up to the fact that — instead of just going for the 'tried and true' 2-3% annual returns — there are ways you can get 6, 8 or even 10% annual income on your investments. Increasing the return you get by just a few percentage points might not sound like a lot, but it is going to make a *huge* difference to your income over time.

CHAPTER 2

USE 'INCOME INVESTING' FOR THE HIGHEST RETURNS

*Build A Comfortable Retirement By Building Up Income Streams
That Pay You — Fast*

* * *

FOR MOST OF YOUR LIFE, YOUR INCOME HAS PROBABLY COME
from your job, where you have to turn up every day, and
where your earning is capped by your position and the
company's policies. As retirement approaches, it's time to
make the switch to relying on your investments to provide
your income.

This can be a daunting process, because there's a lot
riding on this transition — your comfort, security and peace
of mind. You don't just want to build additional income; you
want to build safe, reliable, predictable income.

That's why this isn't a 20-page page article dressed up as a
book, but a complete guide to investing for income the right
way. I want to equip you to build your income on your own
terms — as quickly and safely as possible, to protect your
wealth over both the short- and long-term.

The best option for having a comfortable retirement is to take advantage of compound interest — to invest as early as possible in life to allow your wealth to grow and multiply, so that when you need to start taking income out, you have a bigger base from which to draw. But for many people, this is no longer an option, and so they have to keep exchanging their time for money — they work a job and get a salary in return. That's fine when you're young, but by the time you're in your sixties and seventies, most folks want more time to relax, travel and spend with family.

If that's where you find yourself, income investing is the next best thing. When we talk about income investing, all we're really referring to is choosing investments that will pay you cash on a regular basis, just because you own a little piece of a company or asset.

This is different from speculating on investments.

Most investors choose to buy stocks that they think will go up in price. It's essentially a bet that you will make money on the investment when someone will pay you more later to purchase your shares of stock. In a rising stock market, there's a good chance that could happen — the company might launch a new product, or grow their earnings, or get more market share — but for someone who is depending on their investments to pay their bills, that model is not necessarily going to provide them with safe and steady income.

My colleague Steve Mauzy likes to remind me that "income investing *is* investing. Everything else is simply speculation." What he means is that when you make an investment, you need a return to reward you for the risk you take (and the delayed access to your money). Collecting income regularly is the best way to ensure you end up in a better position than when you started.

This is why income investing is so powerful: it ensures a

return on your money, rather than leaving you guessing about what your monthly income is going to be. It can provide income stability, which gives you the freedom and flexibility to spend your time on what matters most to you (instead of having to spend your 'retirement' working part-time or even having to go back to full-time work to make ends meet).

With the right tools and mindset, there are dozens of ways you can generate additional income for retirement, and you don't need to be a financial genius to make it happen.

The reason many people don't make it happen is that they approach income investment with a limited view of their choices. They think their only options are money market accounts (like 401ks), bonds, and blue chip dividend stocks.

That's really the limit of what most people are familiar with (or comfortable with), but those vehicles are only a fraction of what's available. Often, this is because their own financial advisers or fund managers don't really know how to handle income investing, and that's where I come in.

WARNING: DON'T EVER LAUNCH AN INVESTMENT RESEARCH COMPANY DURING A NATIONAL CRISIS...

I launched Wyatt Investment Research in 2001. My goal was to create a completely independent investment research company that was focused on delivering results for regular investors — not the super wealthy. Little did I know it, but this was one of the worst times I could have chosen to launch... it was just two weeks before the 9/11 terrorist attacks.

Despite the terrible timing, Wyatt Investment Research hit a nerve. In the following years, I grew the audience for our research to over 400,000 daily readers. We've been named #185 on the Inc. 500 list of the fastest growing companies, we were added to the Deloitte Fast 500 list, and we got here because we deliver real results for our customers.

Our independent insights have helped thousands of regular Americans to start building unlimited income, and as a result, my ideas have been shared in *Barron's Magazine*, *MarketWatch.com* from *The Wall Street Journal*, *SeekingAlpha*, *Yahoo! Finance*, and *Kiplinger's Personal Finance Magazine*.

But I've been immersed in investing my whole life. When I was 6 years old, my grandparents gave each of their grandchildren a few shares of Exxon stock. At the time, Exxon was the biggest company in the world, and it was the only stock my grandparents owned. It came out of John D. Rockefeller's Standard Oil, and when I was growing up, it was as famous and successful as Apple is today.

My grandparents weren't wealthy — my granddad was a salesman and my grandmother was a teacher — but they wanted to give each of us a few shares of Exxon to help pay for college and get started on building a secure financial future. I found out about this stock I owned when I was 7 or 8 years old, and right from the start, I thought it was pretty darn interesting.

Whenever we drove the 3 hours to my grandparents' house in Vermont, Grandpa would be sitting on the front porch, reading an investment magazine called *Barron's*. I'd climb up to sit with him and he would tell me about all kinds of investments, and even at that age, these conversations got me really interested in the idea that you could own a small piece of a company. It just seemed so cool to me — I *own* a bit of that Exxon gas station on the corner? Every time we would drive past an Exxon property I would beam a little bit, proud to own something so big and tangible.

When my parents saw that this interest in investing

wasn't a passing phase, they started buying me the *Wall Street Journal*'s guide to investing.

When I was 10 years old I convinced them to let me sell half of my Exxon shares and open up a Charles Schwab account. (At the time, Schwab was one of the few discount brokers and there wasn't any Internet, so if you wanted to buy a stock, you called an 800 number and told the person on the other end of the line what you wanted.) My parents weren't big investors — my dad worked at a university, and my mom was a teacher — but they had friends who were, so when their friends came over for dinner, Mom and Dad would encourage me to talk about my investments.

I subscribed to *Fortune* magazine, and *Barron's*, and I took some of that Exxon money and started buying stocks. I bought Disney, and Topps Baseball Cards, and at the time Tootsie Roll was publicly traded so I got some of that too. As a kid I loved these companies, and I loved that you could buy a bit of their success without working. As I got older and started mowing lawns and delivering papers, any money I earned went into the Schwab account so I could invest more. I was just hooked.

By the time I was in high school, the Internet was really taking off, so I started a website about investing. A lot of investment professionals were sharing their ideas in forums, so I started republishing their research and insights on my website and created one of the first email newsletters focused on investing.

At the time, around 1998, most people were just getting their first email address, and if you put up an email box on your website, folks *loved* the idea of getting something in their inbox. I was among the first people to publish invest-ment content online, which meant that my site became a central source of information for people who were looking for good ideas and ways to manage their money independently.

After I graduated high school, I moved to upstate New York to study economics. But by that time, my little online publishing company was in full swing. After a year, I realized I wanted to focus on doing my own research, making my own investments, and growing my company, so I left school and moved to Washington, D.C. to focus entirely on building the business.

20 years later, there's nothing I could have learned in school or an MBA program that I haven't figured out through actual experience. With enough time, most anybody could learn the same things I have. But time is the one thing most people don't have. My huge advantage is that I started to learn decades before most people even start to think about investing. When they finally have the time, it's usually much later in life, and they've lost years of opportunity.

And if that's where you find yourself, it's not your fault. Investing is scary and overwhelming for a lot of people. There are no investing classes in high school; schools don't even teach basic personal finance. There's nothing like that in college either.

Even if you study economics, they're not teaching you how to invest or manage your own money. If you study business management, they might teach you how to run the finances for a business, but they're not teaching you how to plan your own financial future. This lack of financial education is one of the biggest challenges facing Americans of all ages today, and so one of the key motivations for this book is to distill everything I've learned over that long period of time and empower you to take control of this vital piece of your life.

I want to enable you to understand the most important parts so you can put the information to work — without having to spend years learning it all yourself. I fundamentally believe that you are the best person to manage your own money. If you want to be financially successful and to have a secure retirement, you have to be in charge of your financial destiny.

In the same way you can't outsource your relationship with your spouse and you can't outsource your parenting, you can't outsource building your financial future. You have to own it. Sure, you can hire advisers, buy books, and subscribe to newsletters. But ultimately *you* are in charge of your financial future.

And like you, most folks are willing to do what it takes — you *want* to do the work to be financially secure and successful, but you might not know what the actual process is. You just need a bit of help up front to work out where to start and to build up some momentum until you're ready to keep rolling on your own.

In America, if you have a lot of money already, it's pretty easy to get good advice and support on how to manage your finances. But if you don't have a lot of money, it's almost impossible. No financial adviser wants to take a client who has less than $100,000 (and those that *will* take a client with less aren't the type of financial adviser you want to hire).

A lot of people find themselves stuck here: trying to figure out how they can hit their goals and how they can get good advice, but they don't have enough wealth to get the advice they need, and after all the financial scandals of the past few decades, don't want to put their savings in the hands of someone they don't know or trust.

And to be honest, I can't blame them. A recent study from *The Financial Times* found that mutual fund managers — who invest hundreds of millions or even billions of dollars on behalf of their clients — found that about 50% of fund managers don't invest any of their own money into the fund they manage.[1]

They don't put *any* of their own money where they are putting their clients' money! Why would you let someone put your family's money into investments they don't trust with their own wealth? It's a huge disconnect between the financial services industry and regular folks. And just as importantly, many professional money managers never perform any better than simply matching the market.

They get paid huge salaries to try to beat the market, and they still fall into exactly the same emotional and psychological mistakes as everyone else. In fact, recent data shows that the vast majority of actively managed funds fail to keep up with the S&P 500 index. A recent study from S&P Dow Jones found that over the last decade, 85% of large cap mutual funds failed to keep pace with the S&P 500. And over a period of 15 years, the number increases to 92%.[2]

It's no wonder that mutual fund managers don't want to invest in their own funds!

As best you can, you need to protect your investments against these problems, and so before we get into the actual investment vehicles, we need to talk about one more thing: cultivating the right mindset for income investing.

IF YOU WANT A BRAIN YOU CAN TRUST, USE YOUR OWN: UNPACKING THE INCOME INVESTOR MINDSET

Investing famously requires a cool head, calm heart and the best information you can get your hands on. Unfortunately, even seasoned investors sometimes get overwhelmed by their emotions and fears. That's why it's so important to find sources you can trust to help you make the right decisions for your family's financial health.

This book is designed to teach you everything you need

to know about the most secure income investments available — and to give you all the 'inside knowledge' that most funds and financial investors don't want their customers to know.

Educating yourself financially puts all the power in your hands, and protects you from getting swept up in emotional moments that can lead to financial disasters.

When you don't understand the details of investing, it's so easy to react badly to what's happening in the world. When the news headlines are full of trade wars and rising interest rates and economic downturns, it's completely understandable that you would start to worry. When the markets go down, the numbers in your bank statements go down, and if you don't have the information you need, you will try to get out before the losses get any worse.

Between October and December of 2018, for example, the market went down by 20%. People who were used to seeing $100,000 in their account saw that number go down to $80,000 — and they didn't have the insights they needed to stay the course and protect their wealth. All the news that month was focused on how badly stocks were doing, along with speculation that the downturn could be the start of the next market crash... and people started panicking.

It's understandable, considering all the terrible memories of the financial crisis in 2008 where people lost their homes, and people who thought they were going to retire in 3 years had to work another 10 years to make up for it. In an emotionally tense situation like this, many people make the worst decision possible, and sell all their investments. But what happens then?

Well, after stocks fell 20%, the Federal Reserve changed their tune on interest rates, and stocks went up 20% again. Between October 2018 and March 2019, had you done *nothing*, you would have come out even. But so many people panicked, pulled out all their remaining money, and missed the recovery. And if you miss the recovery, you might not want to buy back in when the prices are so much higher than when you cashed out.

This is what happened after the 2008 recession. Stocks fell almost 50% on the big indexes, and many people sold during the downturn. They were so stressed by the crash that they took too long to get back into the market, and they missed out on the rebound. Many people sat on the sidelines of the markets for years afterwards, waiting to feel confident again, even though the market had already recovered.

The bottom of that crash happened in 2009, and we were still getting emails here in 2015 — *6 years later* — from people who were only just starting to think about getting back into the market after having pulled out at the bottom. The stock prices had gone up 150% by then!

Sadly, it's very common that people will pull out and won't come back for a really long time because they feel like they were burned previously. But the folks who can take a longer view tend to do better. The rollercoaster of emotion is a lot to manage, but the best possible time to be buying is when it feels the worst.

Baron Rothschild, from the Rothschild banking family in Europe, famously said that the time to buy is when there's blood in the streets. When no one else wants to buy anything, because it all looks so bleak, you should be buying as much as you can.

The legendary investor Warren Buffett says the same thing in his shareholder letters. His company, **Berkshire Hathaway (NYSE: BRK-b)**, recently had over $122 billion in cash. That's more than every other company — except **Apple (NASDAQ: AAPL)**.

Why is Warren Buffett holding onto so much cash? It's because he thinks the valuations for companies are too high. In his 2018 annual shareholder letter, Buffett wrote that prices "are sky-high for businesses possessing decent long-term prospects."

Buffett refuses to pay top dollar. Instead, he wants to swoop in when no one else has the money or willingness or conviction to write a check. In times of crisis, they want to support the companies they own, and they want to buy new ones (and buy them at more sensible prices).

While Buffett does not claim to time the market, he does focus on value. When prices are high and valuations are overextended, Berkshire Hathaway tends to let its cash accumulate. And then when the market declines, the company starts aggressively acquiring publicly traded stocks and private companies.

The following chart shows how Berkshire invested nearly $20 billion during the 2008-2009 recession. During a one-year period from December 2007 through December of 2008, the company's cash declined by 45%, dropping from $44.33 billion in cash to $25.54 billion, as Buffett aggressively purchased assets on the cheap.[3]

Critically, guys like Warren Buffett, Fidelity's Peter Lynch and the late Vanguard founder Jack Bogle have said over and over that they don't know how to time the market. They are the best investors in the world, so if *they* can't predict what's going to happen in the market, how on earth can you or I? No one knows what the market is going to do in the short-term, and therefore, it's best to take a long-term view.

Now, I obviously believe that income investing should always be a part of everybody's investment strategy. Your strategy does not need to be built exclusively around income investing, but at least part of your portfolio should pay you some regular income.

It's OK to invest in stocks that don't pay you dividends — for example, I own shares of Google and Facebook, and they don't pay dividends. I own marijuana stocks that don't pay dividends. I'm invested in those things because I think there's a lot of growth potential with those companies and opportunities, but I also want to balance that with dividend stocks that are going to pay me every quarter. It's wise to have a mixed, balanced approach, where your risk is spread out across different types of investment to protect your overall wealth.

That's also not to say that when you are retired you need to be 100% focused on income and avoiding all risk. It's good to keep taking some chances, but as we age, most of us tend to get more conservative in our investments, because we have less time horizon to make up for any losses. That's why people commonly move into more conservative investing positions and more income investments as they prepare for retirement.

As a shareholder in a business, or as an investor who gives capital to someone else, you want to get paid back a little bit all the time. You don't want to write a check and then wait a decade or two to find out if you're going to make some money from it — you feel a lot more comfortable if you get a little piece of the profits every few months. And that's what income investing is all about: getting paid back a little bit of your capital and getting a little bit of profit in your pocket all the time.

In the next chapter, I want to give you a brief overview of all the different investment vehicles we're going to explore, so that you can start using this book to maximize your income. You can either read it through from start to finish, or you can dip into the sections that interest you the most. Use it the way that makes the most sense to you, and that will help you learn most effectively. You don't need any special qualifications to make this information work for you, and you don't need to have a background in economics, finance or business. All you need is the determination to take control of your money and the willingness to learn how. You can reach me any time through our private Facebook group if you have any questions: www.facebook.com/groups/incomeinvestors/.

Let's get started.

CHAPTER 3

"WHERE DO THE RICH REALLY INVEST THEIR MONEY?"

7 Wealth Multipliers The Super Rich Use To Skyrocket Their Wealth, Freedom and Independence

* * *

IF YOU'VE EVER WONDERED WHAT ALL THE RICHEST PEOPLE IN America do with their money, this book will show you many of the most reliable strategies that grow their wealth exponentially over time.

Of course, some folks get rich thanks to an inheritance. But many wealthy Americans are self-made, and they've become so wealthy because they have learned how to make their money work for them.

The rich seem to have an instinct for finding opportunities that grow their wealth. They know how to be in the right place at the right time, with cash in hand or checkbook open. But this is not some special 'sixth sense' you develop when you make your first million. It's information, and in today's economy, information is wealth.

If you're ready to develop your own instincts for building your wealth, let's start shining a light on the income investment strategies the richest people in the country use to multiply their money.

Before we get started, a quick but important note: All investment opportunities carry some inherent risk, and there's a balance to strike between pursuing big opportunities to generate wealth, and protecting the wealth that you already have. You alone can decide what your risk tolerance is, how aggressively you want to invest, and in types of strategy.

But these strategies have proven themselves over and over to be safe, reliable income investments when you approach them with a clear understanding of how they work and what they should be used for. Caveats out of the way, let's dive in.

YOUR UNLIMITED INCOME ROADMAP: DECIDING WHERE TO PUT YOUR MONEY FOR MAXIMUM RETURNS

At the risk of being obvious, when we call something an investment vehicle, we're just referring to the types of investment you can put your money into — stocks are a vehicle, bonds are a vehicle, real estate is a vehicle and so on. An income investment vehicle, specifically, will pay you regular income, usually through a quarterly or annual dividend. A dividend is a payment made to shareholders from the company's profits for that timeframe.

In this book, we're going to cover more than 20 income investment opportunities, and I want to give you a quick overview in the next section, since I know not everyone will have the time to read every single chapter. Sometimes it's useful to know where you can just dip in and get the information you're particularly interested at that moment. Some of these vehicles are big and complex, and have multiple variants.

Others are simple and straightforward, and they carry various levels of risk, but all of them are proven vehicles that will pay you regularly.

You can start investing in any of these vehicles at any time, as it feels appropriate to you. Whether you're just starting out, or already have some of these investments in place, this plan will help you tap into the unlimited options the market has available for income generation.

INVESTMENTS WHICH PREDICTABLY PAY OUT 9% OR MORE...

The first type of income investment we'll explore is called the Business Development Corporation (BDC), which operate like banks, in that they raise money and loan it out to businesses who have not been able to secure funding from regular banks (because they're too small for a bank to bother with, their credit rating isn't high enough, or they're in an uncertain situation). A BDC usually charges higher interest rates, because of this additional risk.

Instead of lending money to giant corporations like Walmart, as a huge bank might, they might lend money to say, a manufacturing company that turns over $100 million a year. If you invested in Wells Fargo or another big bank, the return would usually be around 2%, whereas BDCs are required to pay out a minimum of 90% of its profits to shareholders, so oftentimes, these kinds of investments pay out around 9 or 10%.

That's an income potential of around 5 times what you would get from a traditional investment in the banking space.

Real Estate Investment Trusts (REITs) are another strong income investment. These are funds that invest in real estate, so you get the cash flow from collecting rent on the properties the fund owns, and your capital will appreciate in lockstep with the market if real estate prices go up. There are many different types of REIT, specializing in different types of real estate. Your money is pooled to invest in apartment buildings, healthcare facilities or data storage centers (just a few examples of many potential real estate categories).

REITs are also required to return 90% or more of their profits to shareholders, so this type of investment often creates returns two or three times higher than a typical dividend stock, and you also own the real estate as a back up.

A lot of people like the idea of real estate, because it's physical and known to be a safe bet, but at the same time, most people don't want to buy an apartment building and manage it themselves, so REITs are a great way to get the benefits without all the downside.

A third option is master limited partnerships (MLPs), which are companies that transport or refine energy — oil or natural gas. These companies are not doing any of the exploration or mining; they just own the pipeline that takes the oil from Texas to the Gulf of Mexico, for example, where it's put on their ships to be taken to their refineries and turned into the final, usable product.

The energy industry isn't glamorous, but it's essential: we all put gas in our cars, we all need power in our homes, so these companies are protected from fluctuations that can affect other companies in this sector. Whether oil prices are high or low, the oil companies still need to have it transported and refined.

MLPs are stable investments that are also required to pay 90% or more of their profits to shareholders, and often have yields of 8 to 10%, much higher than the standard 2% yield from a regular stock.

Next up, we'll delve into the Dogs of the Dow. This is a perfect strategy for the individual investor who doesn't want to spend much time researching companies and adjusting their portfolio.

Basically, you buy a selection of stocks from the Dow Jones (determined by a simple set of criteria), right at the end of the year. You hold them all year, collecting the highest returns from all the companies listed on the index, and repeat the process at the end of the following year. These returns vary, based on the performance of the companies on the index, but you can expect returns of up to 5 or 6%.

Next up are the Dividend Achievers and Aristocrats. These are companies that have increased the dividends paid to investors every single year, for 10 years and 25 years respectively. The yields on these stocks is often not as high as we see from other investments in this book, but because the dividends increase every year, you get a compounding effect — both the value of your initial capital increases, as does the percentage yield you receive each year.

Floating rate funds function in a similar way to BDCs, loaning money to companies that regular banks won't fund. However, where BDCs have fixed rate loans, floating rate funds have variable interest rates. That means that if interest rates go up, the rates on all their loans go up too.

Floating rate funds are exposed to a bit more volatility than other investments, which means that their yields are generally higher than other funds too — the higher the risk, the higher the reward. That's not to say that floating rate funds overall are risky, just that a small percentage of their loans are.

Selling options is a common strategy among professional

investors but often seems out of reach for the individual investor. That's a shame, because you can drastically increase the amount of money you earn from any given stock by selling options on it.

We're going to discuss two types of options — covered calls and puts — where another investor pays you a fee for the right to buy your stock or to sell you stock, and that have major potential for you to acquire quality stocks at better-than-market prices.

Next, we'll look at Warren Buffett's exceptional investment strategy at his company, Berkshire Hathaway. Since Berkshire Hathaway doesn't pay dividends to their shareholders, we'll break down how you can get all the benefit of his investment expertise *and* get paid on a regular basis, by choosing companies in his portfolio that do pay dividends.

Liberty Checks are a little-known strategy for private investors. Also known as special dividends, these are one-time payments made by large companies that have amassed too much cash on their balance sheets and want to return it to their shareholders.

Here at Wyatt Research we focus on Liberty Checks that will pay a 4% yield at the minimum, but we've seen these special dividends pay out as much as 40%. There is an important 'buy and hold' element to maximizing the benefit of this strategy, but we're seeing a Liberty Check that meets our criteria come in around every 3 weeks — a major opportunity to bring in extra cash.

We'll also look at gold royalties, and how you can take advantage of a very stable asset without all the hassle and mismanagement that has historically been a big downside to this investment.

Finally, we'll look at two ways you can ditch your conventional bank account with its paltry return, and put that money to much better use. One strategy is a special account that pays over 300% more interest than regular accounts, and another is to put your money into a peer-to-peer lending account, where you essentially get rid of the bank to lend small amounts to other people of your choosing, who will then pay you higher interest rates for those loans.

EXPANDING YOUR INVESTMENTS

In the last section of the book, we're going to explore some strategies you can use to compound the earnings you receive from the investments you choose.

We'll talk about dividend reinvestment programs (DRIPs), that allow you to automatically buy more stock with your dividend payments, rather than receiving them as cash. We'll also look at 893(C) funds — also known as closed-end funds, these funds generally pay 2 or 3 times the amount of a regular stock — and preferred stocks are another way to get paid greater dividends on your stock holdings.

Solar investment is another big opportunity. While there's a sizeable upfront investment to shift your home's energy source to solar, there are major tax breaks associated with it, and the savings on your energy bills are so significant that within a few years, you're essentially making money by harvesting sunshine (often to the tune of 12 to 15% annually of your original investment).

We'll also look at owning rental properties. While there is a lot more work to do when when you manage rentals yourself, it can be a great way to generate income, particularly if you're confident in your own skills to do repairs and maintenance. While this isn't going to be feasible for everyone, if it fits with your circumstances, you can expect to see a healthy return on your investment, often 5 to 7% each year.

GETTING PAST FEAR & DOUBT BY MASTERING THE ECONOMIC CYCLE

If you want to invest the right way, and do so often, it's important to limit the 'knee jerk' reactions so many people fall into when it comes to protecting and growing their money. Failure to do this can cause you to lose a small fortune, and delay the growth of your wealth by months or even years.

In order to protect your investments (and your sanity), it's important to understand the economic cycle and interest rates. We're not going to get into huge detail here, but if you understand the big picture, you're going to be in a good position to identify what's happening (and why) in the economic environment at any given time.

This will empower you to make better decisions about what to do with your money and will hopefully protect you from making some of the emotional mistakes that many investors (including the professionals) fall into so often.

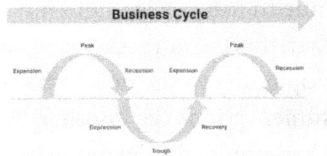

At the beginning of the economic cycle, you have gradual expansion, where economic growth is increasing, then a peak. This process generally takes 4 or 5 years, and then is followed by recession, where economic growth is declining. This usually lasts a couple of years too.

Recessions are not always severe — often it's just a downturn — but if it is severe, we will see a depression, which is the lowest point possible in an economic cycle. The 2008 crash was a major recession, but it wasn't a depression (the last time that happened was the Great Depression of 1929-1939, when there was outright despair that lasted for a decade). We often we skip depression and just go back to the start — from recession to expansion.

This is basically a cycle of expansion and contraction. You have periods where the economy is doing well and people are feeling prosperous, things are going great, and then you have periods when the rate of growth is slowing.

When the economy is doing really well, people want to invest for growth, they want to invest in risky things. They might be interested right now for example in marijuana stocks, or cryptocurrencies, or biotechnology stocks — growth sectors that give them much more exposure to upside, since they're not too worried about the downside.

The opposite is true during a recession — during slower times investors tend to seek the most security and safety for their money and want to get out of anything that seems risky. Often those options are oriented more towards income — sectors that are essentially recession-proof.

People continue to use services and buy products in these categories whether there is a recession or not. Healthcare is one (you don't skip going to the doctor because the economy is weak). Consumer goods is another (you keep buying toothpaste and shampoo and food, no matter what happens).

These sectors are called consumer staple goods — they are part of the essential fabric of our lives and tend to do better than consumer discretionary goods during a down-turn. For example, you might be less likely to shop at Nordstrom if you're feeling less financially secure, or you might be less likely to buy a new car — as much as you might *want* a new car, you're likely to put that purchase off because your current car is doing fine. It's not a necessity and you can put it off until later when you're feeling more confident about the financial future.

When people are seeking safety and security, they want to invest in companies they know and trust. They want to know that even if stock prices don't go up in the next year, they'll get a return on their investment through income. They tend to favor stocks that have consistent profits and are able to grow, even a little bit, during a recession — companies that don't have a lot of debt and won't need to issue more debt in order to fund their operations. They tend to favor Fortune 500 companies, companies on the S&P 500, like Walmart, McDonalds, Verizon, Microsoft and so on.

We don't worry that companies like these are overleveraged, are not going to be able to pay their bills or will lose their business entirely, so we trust them when things are looking shaky.

It's often easier to see the signs of an economic expansion than the signs of economic contraction. When times are good, there are all kinds of signs you can observe in everyday life.

Unemployment rates go down, and lots of jobs are available. Restaurants are busy and cinemas are full. Your friends are buying houses and cars, and when Apple launches a new iPhone, it's immediately back- ordered for 6 weeks. When people are spending plenty of money, that's a good sign that the economy is expanding.

It can take a bit longer to notice the signs that a recession is coming. You can look at the rate of temporary employment agencies — if those companies are struggling, it's a sign that companies aren't overwhelmed with work and don't need temps to help them out. Shipping and trucking performance can be another one — if those industries are slowing it can be a sign that there's less economic activity happening.

For example, when FedEx announces that they are seeing a downturn in international shipping (coinciding with a trade war or tariff conflict, for example), then 3 months later, we will usually see economic data that reflects that slowdown — FedEx was just first to notice this, because they're right in the middle of it, rather than at the edges where the data is collected.

Low unemployment is obviously good news, but it can also be a sign that a downturn is on the horizon. At a certain point, the wages start increasing because there's more competition for workers. This puts the worker in a good position but also raises the costs for the business to operate, which cuts down profit margins.

The US often undergoes a recession 9-12 months after the unemployment level reaches its lowest point. Really low unemployment (below 4%) is a really good sign that we're at the peak of an economic cycle. Now, we might stay at that peak for a while — it's not like there's some trigger that causes a downturn as soon as you hit that high; we could stay at that peak for a year or more.

In 2007, right before the 2008 recession, unemployment was just over 4%, which was the lowest it had been since 2001. It's hard to know what the low point of unemployment is going to be until you can look back with hindsight, but historically low unemployment tends to indicate a recession might be coming in the next year or two.

If we're at the peak of an economic cycle, and you think a recession could be coming soon, it can be a good moment to recalibrate your portfolio. Obviously, the best time to prepare for a downturn is before it happens, and that means trying to be a bit more defensive in your investments.

The way you would do that is to rotate out of your riskier investments and into safer ones. You may decide to focus on things that hold their value — things like cash and gold (which may go up in the face of falling equity prices).

Ray Dalio, the chair and chief investment officer of Bridgewater Associates, the biggest hedge fund in the world, recommends holding 5 to 10% of your portfolio in gold to protect yourself against downturns in the market:

"If you don't have 5-10% of your assets in gold as a hedge, we'd suggest that you relook at this. Don't let traditional biases, rather than an excellent analysis, stand in the way of you doing this."[1]

We'll talk about how gold investments can be an income-producing strategy, in addition to providing increased security, later in the book.

One of the good things about income investing is that it's a bellwether strategy — it works in any environment. In times of economic uncertainty, it becomes even more popular. When the stock market is going up 10% every year, people tend to be less interested in earning income, because it's kind of boring. It's more exciting to invest in the next Facebook or Google and people tend to prioritize investing in hot stocks that are climbing higher and higher, thinking they'll just sell some stocks if they need income.

But when the market is moving sideways or going down, people think more about protecting their money and the downside risks. Companies that pay dividends and reward their shareholders tend to be viewed as more safe and stable, because they're profitable, and they actually have cash on hand.

Dividends don't lie — either a company has the cash to

pay their shareholders, or they don't. Companies can't fake this like they can fake other 'evidence' of success. When you look at all the financial fraud that has happened over the years — with Enron and WorldComm and many companies more recently — you can see that accountants can manipulate income statements and cash flow statements. They can increase the earnings per share by depreciating assets a certain way, or booking revenues in a different way or accelerating the recognition of this or that, but dividends really can't be manipulated like that.

Either the company pays you cash or it doesn't, so in times of uncertainty, income investing is a strategy that provides a lot of security and confidence to smart investors.

They say that bull markets don't die of old age — it's not like economic growth just stops; typically something changes that causes a slow-down. And if you look at what sparks a recession, historically, it's been that the Federal Reserve has raised interest rates too aggressively at the wrong point in the economic cycle. The Federal Reserve has caused more recessions this way than any other cause, and that's why investors pay so much attention to what's going on with interest rates.

HOW SHIFTING INTEREST RATES CAN AFFECT YOUR INVESTMENTS

Rising interest rates, by themselves, are not an indicator of a slowing economy. When the Fed raises rates, they're indicating that the economy is doing well enough that we can support those higher rates. When a raise is done correctly, it's a sign that the economy is in great shape, and can be good news for investors — you're going to earn more money on the deposits you have in the bank, and on your bonds and equities.

For example, if you're investing in bonds and interest rates go up, any newly issued bonds would have higher interest rates attached to them as well. If the Fed raises rates from 2% to 4%, then newly issued bonds would pay twice as much.

The downside is that if the rate goes up and you already own bonds, the value of your bond goes down when interest rates go up — they move in inverse. This is why a lot of investors are hesitant to buy long-duration bonds, or any type of fixed income investment (whether it's Federal Reserve, corporate, or municipal), when interest rates are low.

The issue is that one of the Fed's main tools to ease the effects of a downturn is to cut interest rates. It cuts the cost of borrowing for consumers and businesses — this makes money cheap, and the cheaper money is, the more people borrow to buy cars and houses and so on. It's an important tool for the Federal Reserve to have when the economy isn't doing well, but the Fed will often overshoot and raise rates too quickly, too far, or at the wrong time.

The conundrum is that sometimes we reach a late stage in the economic cycle and the Fed hasn't raised the interest rates in a while, which leaves them without any viable options to ease a downturn.

For example, at the time of writing this book, we were pretty late in the economic cycle. I was confident that a recession was on the horizon within the next 12-18 months, but the interest rate at the time was only 2%. The Fed should have been raising rates much more aggressively over the past few years, since we were in an economic boom, but they didn't.

In December of 2018, they were talking about doing a couple of rate increases during 2019, but by the middle of 2019, they were talking about making two cuts to rates instead. Growth had started slowing, and it was too late — the Federal Reserve couldn't justify raising rates anymore. And if things progress into a recession, they don't have much ability to cut rates because they are already artificially low. It's a stark contrast to their predictions from a year ago and I think a good sign that a downturn is coming.

Now, because we don't know when rates are going to go up or down, one of the best options we have to mitigate that uncertainty is to make investments that are not necessarily correlated to interest rates, and in companies that don't have a lot of debt and are therefore not exposed to changes in rates.

A lot of the dividend stocks we are going to cover in this book fit this profile — they are big companies that are very profitable, have lots of cash, and consistently reward their shareholders. If interest rates go up, they're going to be unaffected and will continue to have a good business. That's why it's also important to understand the numbers associated with these types of investments, and the difference between dividend growth and dividend yield is a big one.

DIVIDEND GROWTH VERSUS DIVIDEND YIELD

Here's the scoop on how to find truly valuable companies which pay you regular income over time, and how to identify which companies are the safest and most reliable places to put your money.

When we talk about dividend stocks, a lot of people will focus on the yield of a stock. If they were looking at two different stocks, purely from an income standpoint, and one had a yield of 2% and the other a yield of 4%, they might say to themselves, "Well, these are similar companies, and since one has a yield that's double the other, that must be the better company." The same could be true when assessing a real estate investment trust (REIT), master limited partnership (MLP), business development company (BDC), or any kind of stock. But the dividend yield and dividend growth are two different things, and this is key for income investors to understand.

We tend to find that companies with higher yields have little or no growth in their dividends. A high yield often indicates that they are not increasing their dividend payments, whereas stocks with dividend growth typically have a lower yield percentage.

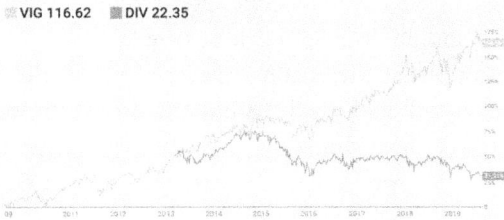

Apple is a good example of this — every year Apple increases its dividend by 10%. It might only be a 2% dividend, but every year the dividend amount grows by 10% of the original amount (it goes from 2% to 2.2%, to 2.4% and so on). What typically happens is that the stock price of these dividend growers, as they're called, will go up in lockstep with the increase in dividends over time. That means if the company increases its dividend by 10% per year, over a long period of time, the share price will typically be highly correlated with that dividend increase.

So if a company like Apple increases its payments by 10% per year, and they're paying 2% in dividends, you could be looking at a 12% total return from the stock. Large blue-chip companies often increase their dividends every year as a way to reward shareholders and let them share in the profits.

Smart investors are willing to sacrifice yield today for the sake of future growth in the yield payments. It's really important to understand that some of the best income investments are not those with high yields — a low yield with a growing dividend distribution can be a much better investment.

The reason is that if a company is growing its payments by, say, 10% a year, over time, your total yield from that will increase as well. The second important part is that when companies grow their distributions, the share price tends to move in tandem with that over the long term. So if over the next 7 years, Microsoft doubles its dividend payment, the stock price should double in price as well.

For example, if Microsoft today yields 2%, then 7 years from now, it will still yield 2% but the dollar amount of the payments will have doubled — maybe the stock has gone from paying $1 per share to $2 per share, even though the yield as a percentage has stayed the same.

Of course, this doesn't always work perfectly — there are cycles in the economy, companies go in and out of favor, people value stocks differently in the future, so it's not 100% certain, but you can expect companies that are consistently growing their dividends to see their share prices appreciate, whereas the companies that don't share their dividends often won't see much growth in their stock price.

Some of the BDCs are a good example of this. Some of these companies pay out a very high yield of greater than 9%. Yet over the past 10 years, the stock prices of many BDCs have gone nowhere. That doesn't make these high-yield BDCs a bad investment — from an income standpoint, you're getting large and regular payments — all it means is that the size of those payments is not increasing and your principal investment is not appreciating over time. It's just important to understand that higher yield doesn't always mean better investment or a higher total return.

There's also a real risk in chasing yield. Chasing yield is when someone looks at their income needs, and ends up backing themselves into a number that they need their portfolio to produce.

Let's say you have $100,000 in a portfolio, and you feel that you need to be earning $6,000 in annual income from your portfolio to meet your expenses. That would mean you need to have an average yield across the portfolio of 6%, so you let the yield dictate what you buy, rather than letting the quality of the company dictate the right investments.

If there's a specific number you need, you might be better off buying lots of stocks that yield 4% but are growing their dividend payments.

It's important to be extremely cautious when investing in high-yield stocks paying out over 10%. When a company has a very high yield, it can be an indication that there's a problem in their business. If a company has a 12 or 15% yield, it may mean that the stock price has gotten beaten up and the company hasn't yet cut their dividend payments and when they do, the yield will fall. If they are forced to cut their dividend payments in half, say, your 12% yield will go to 6%.

The stock price is telling you that the market thought this was going to happen, but novice investors often get suckered into buying this kind of stock, just by looking purely at the high yield.

To be clear, some of my favorite income investments and companies in this book have very high yields. But these are companies we've vetted extensively and believe to be low-risk. They have been thriving for many years, and have proven themselves over long periods to be stable, well-managed companies.

Many of them are also structured in such a way that they

are *required* to return nearly all of their profits to investors, unlike private companies who want to hold on to as much profit as possible. So now that you have a firm foundation about economic cycles, interest rates and the balance between dividend yield and dividend growth, let's get started.

CHAPTER 4

COLLECT 10X MORE INCOME FROM SECRET 'OFF WALL STREET' BANKS

Get Access To The Deals Your Local Branch Will Never Give You

* * *

THE NEXT TIME YOU WALK INTO YOUR LOCAL BANK (OR GO online), take a look at the interest you're earning on your savings.

These days, most banks are paying just 1% on a typical savings account or certificate of deposit (CD). And that means even if you have $100,000 in savings... you're only earning $1,000 in *annual* income. That's just $83 per month.

Frankly, it's a little insulting. Your money should be delivering *much* more income than that — and you don't have to settle for that kind of lousy return. That's why BDCs are such a popular income investment — many of them are paying out 5 to 10 times more income than the average savings account.

These "off Wall Street banks" do business a little differently to the institution that holds your cash for you. Created by the US Congress in 1980, BDCs were designed to boost job growth and to help emerging companies acquire the funds they need to grow.

While traditional banks deal directly with individual customers looking to manage their money, BDCs focus on providing loans to small and medium-sized businesses. Many traditional banks and credit providers often won't deal with these companies, because they are not as credit-worthy as other companies the banks could invest in.

These constraints are of less concern to BDCs, since they generally offer financing to companies at a higher interest rate than a conventional bank would offer. These higher interest rate loans allow BDCs to offset the credit risk by paying more generous dividends.

Additionally, many BDCs issue floating rate loans. That means that if the Federal Reserve raises the interest rate by 0.25%, the interest rate on the BDC's loans will also be raised 0.25%. This ensures that the BDC and its investors continue to be compensated fairly for the higher risk they are accommodating in this investment and helps protect them from the risk of rising interest rates.

Most of the loans BDCs make are called senior secured loans. This structure means that this particular debt takes priority over any unsecured debt. Let's say that John owns a chain of eyeglass clinics in Illinois. He needs additional capital to expand his operation, so a BDC makes him a senior secured loan. The terms of this loan say that this debt to him will be guaranteed by the other assets of the business.

So if John defaults on his payments, all the assets of the business (like property, machinery and so on) will be sold and the BDC will be repaid first from the proceeds, ahead of any other lenders.

Of course, no BDC wants to see one of their companies default, so they tend to be quite involved in the companies they invest in. Unlike a conventional bank, which hands over the money and leaves the company to its own devices, BDCs operate more akin to private equity firms. For example, if John's business is valued at $100 million, and a BDC wrote him a check for $20 million, they might take a seat on his board of directors, or meet with him every quarter to check in on how the business is doing.

There's no hard rule about this, but given the amount of money BDCs are typically investing, it's common for them to be fairly hands-on in guiding the company forward. This is prudent for the BDC, beneficial to the company's growth, and ultimately good for the individual investor too — investments tend to perform better when things are transparent and subject to regular attention and accountability.

GET BACK-DOOR ACCESS TO HUNDREDS OF WEALTH OPPORTUNITIES THROUGH A SINGLE INVESTMENT

When you harness Business Development Companies, you are not limited by your net worth, income or other restrictions which might have handcuffed you in the past. Investing in BDCs is similar to investing in a venture capital fund, without the restrictions from the government that require accreditation, income and net worth restrictions and so on. You buy one stock in the BDC, and you get exposure to the growth of dozens (if not hundreds) of companies through their investments.

BDCs are known as 'pass-through entities' — they are allowed to avoid paying federal income taxes, *if* they distribute 90% of the profits to shareholders. Most C-Corporations pay federal income taxes, then income

distributed to shareholders (in the form of dividends) is taxed again at the personal level. This means that income generated by most corporations is taxed twice by the time investors receive their dividends.

But because BDCs are exempt from the federal income taxes, the income they are able to distribute to shareholders is often much higher than other types of investments (and because they offer floating rate terms, they're also less likely than other investments to be impacted by increases in federal interest rates).

This means that BDCs pay generous dividends to their shareholders. If you're investing for income, BDCs pay out *huge* amounts compared to normal banks, and can provide significant amounts of extra cash on a regular basis. For example, the **UBS Business Development Company ETF (NYSE: BDCZ)** pays out 8.6% dividends. This number is a reflection of the average BDC, since the ETF invests in over 40 different BDCs. That's a hefty return compared to the ~1% dividends from the big banks!

The following table shows the yields from BDCs compared with big banks. You can see that BDCs typically yield two to three times more income than you'd collect from a typical bank stock.

Business Development Companies	Ticker	Share Price	Yield
UBS ETRACS Wells Fargo Business Development Company ETN	NYSE: BDC	$19.67	8.7%
Ares Capital	NASDAQ: ARCC	18.57	8.5
Saratoga Investment Company	NYSE: SAR	25.17	8.5
Apollo Investment Corporation	NASDAQ: AINV	16.35	11.1
TPG Specialty Lending Company	NYSE: TSLX	19.52	7.5
Big Banks	**Ticker**	**Share Price**	**Yield**
SPDR S&P Bank ETF	NYSE: KBE	$44.77	2.2%
Wells Fargo	NYSE: WFC	45.00	4.6
Bank of America	NYSE: BAC	26.93	2.7
BB&T	NYSE: BBT	51.53	3.9

Source: Morningstar. All data as of 7/31/19.

When you're looking to buy into a BDC, a key factor to assess is how consistent they are with their payments to shareholders. It's a big red flag if they are inconsistent with payments — up one quarter, down the next, up one quarter, down the next — because it shows they're not earning consistent levels of income.

Another thing to look at is whether they are being forced to write off loans. If they make a loan of $100 million, for example, and then are eventually forced to write down the value of that loan to $50 million (due to a risk that the company is going to default on payment at the higher amount), it might be a sign they're not doing enough due diligence or oversight on their investments.

Most BDCs also put out regular press releases detailing new loans they are committing to and exits they are making. Just like other publicly traded companies, BDCs report their earnings every 3 months. Those earnings reports reveal lots of important information (how much money the company earned, what the dividend payment is going to be, the current value of the investments in their portfolio, how has that changed over the last year etc.), and so you essentially get an insight into the financial health of the BDC — and therefore the companies they're invested in — every quarter.

As with any type of investment, choosing a high-quality BDC is extremely important. Focus on investing with BDCs that have a long operating history, and have had lots of success. Smart people don't just get dumb overnight, so hedge your bets by investing in BDCs led by management teams who have a long track record of being successful.

There's no minimum amount that a private shareholder needs to invest in order to access BDCs — the cost of entry is based purely on the share price. If it's trading at $10 a share, you could conceivably buy just one share and start with that. That makes it much more accessible than a mutual fund, for example, which might have a minimum of $1,000 to open an account.

While they are individual companies, BDCs offer exposure to hundreds of different companies that you wouldn't be able to access on your own. You don't have to make a choice about which of the BDC's companies you want your money to go to, and once you've bought the BDC stock, you reap the benefits of all of the companies they are invested in.

Before we wrap up this chapter, I want to give you the inside scoop on one of the best BDCs operating in the country today.

BEYOND THE S&P 500: GET 9X MORE RETURN THAN YOUR TYPICAL SAVINGS ACCOUNT.

One of my favorite BDCs is **Ares Capital (NASDAQ: ARCC)**. Ares is the biggest BDC in the country, and I would argue, the most successful. As of this writing, Ares was yielding over 9% — more than 4 times that of the average company listed on the S&P 500. Plus, it pays out 9 times more income than the typical savings account.

That's a *big* difference in income returns. Note, though, that investors in BDCs should not expect a great deal of capital growth. For instance, over the past 5 years Ares Capital's stock price has largely remained stable — not losing much and not gaining much.

The focus of Ares and most other BDCs is to provide an attractive income stream for investors rather than to create significant capital appreciation. Of course, this is the same for any bank: depositing your money into a savings account doesn't give you any real capital gains either, so a BDC like Ares puts you significantly ahead on your income than you would be otherwise.

Founded in 1997, ARCC is the largest business development company in the country by both market capitalization (the total dollar market value of a company's outstanding shares) and total assets, with approximately $13.8 billion of total assets. Their investment portfolio generates a 14% internal rate of return (IRR) , and they've been paying a 12% annual shareholder return since their IPO in 2004.

At the time of writing, ARCC's portfolio consists of 345 portfolio companies, backed by 163 different private equity sponsors. The portfolio is diversified across multiple asset classes, industries, and geographic locations.

Here's a quick breakdown of how their assets are divided across industries:

- Healthcare Services: 19.9%
- Business Services: 18.8%
- Consumer Products: 7.2%
- Senior Direct Lending Program: 7.1%
- Financial Services: 6.1%
- Power Generation: 6%
- Other Services: 5.1%
- Manufacturing: 4.9%
- Automotive Services: 4.1%
- Restaurants and Food Services: 3.4%
- Food and Beverage: 3.4%
- Oil and Gas: 3.4%
- Wholesale Distribution: 2.1%
- Education: 1.9%
- Containers and Packaging: 1.7%
- Remaining: 4.9%[1]

Over 73% of Ares' loans are senior secured loans, so even though the risk profile is higher than what a conventional bank might see, the downside is limited and the payoff is consistently much higher. Ares has stable investment grade ratings from Moody's, S&P Global and Fitch Ratings, their annual loss rate is significantly better than the industry average, and has generated cumulative core earnings and net realized gains in excess of the dividends paid since their IPO.

CHAPTER 5

LOOPHOLE CREATES VENTURE CAPITAL FIRM
PAYING 9.9%

*Skip The Red Tape To Take Advantage Of Silicon Valley's Best
Investments*

* * *

VENTURE CAPITAL INVESTMENTS HAVE USUALLY BEEN OFF
limits to the majority of the public — except for those of us
with really deep pockets.

Before now, only about 3% of all investors in the US
could get their hands on these opportunities to surge their
wealth and get income rolling in regularly.

Venture capital firms are specifically designed to invest in
promising private companies, and aim to buy a sizeable stake
of the equity by investing in the early stages. And when these
private companies go public — or get acquired — they can
cash out huge profits.

Unfortunately, the best venture capital firms aren't accessible for roughly 97% of investors, because they can only
accept investments from "accredited investors" with a net
worth of greater than $1 million (or $200,000 in annual

income). Plus, most of these funds often require a minimum investment of $1 million to $5 million.

But there's a loophole that levels the playing field for regular folks who just want a fair shot at enjoying the same type of rewards the ultra-wealthy have been raking in for years: a BDC that operates like a venture capital fund, investing in cutting-edge technology, life sciences and renewable technologies — **Hercules Capital (NYSE: HTGC).**

Located in Silicon Valley, Hercules focuses on investing in early-stage growth companies. The company maintains an investment portfolio in the range of $1.3 billion to $1.6 billion in mid-sized businesses, primarily through structured debt and equity holdings.

Hercules' model opens up investment possibilities for people who are prohibited from investing in conventional venture capital companies. Because they are a BDC but *operate* like a venture capital fund, they are able to make these exciting deals available to regular investors.

You can invest in Hercules and gain an indirect owner-ship stake in those private companies, without needing to participate in any IPOs or compete with other investors when their stock is publicly traded, or to have huge amounts of capital at your disposal.

Hercules devotes a lot of its attention and capital to privately-held growth businesses — funding companies like Ancestry.com, FanDuel (one of the country's largest daily fantasy sports sites), Sling Media (a content streaming company), and BrightSource Energy, which finances, builds and operates utility-scale solar power plants.

They also invested in Facebook before the IPO: a report in the *Wall Street Journal* said that Facebook's IPO would be 'unprecedented' in the history of venture capital, with experts weighing in to say that it might have been "the single best venture investment ever." It's no surprise that Hercules wanted to get in on this deal, and they acquired 307,500 shares of Facebook. Hercules CEO Manuel Henriquez said, "It would be absolutely insane to be in Silicon Valley and not have some participation in what's likely to be the largest IPO in the venture-capital industry."[1]

Participating in Facebook's IPO would have been difficult for many private investors, but this loophole in Hercules' set-up made it available to all their shareholders regardless of how much money they had available.

These kinds of deals can significantly contribute to the amount of income a BDC can pay its shareholders, and Hercules Capital has enjoyed both strong asset and income growth in the years since the 2008-2009 recession. At a time when conventional banks were a little gun-shy about funding riskier industries, Hercules consistently made smart bets about financing the development of promising companies.

Like other BDCs, it then worked closely with those companies to grow their success (and continues to do so), with an eventual goal of the company being acquired or going public through an initial public offering.

Hercules also differs from other BDCs in how it makes returns to investors. Most BDCs rely on dividend payouts to return profit to investors, and any capital appreciation is very limited, but that's not the case with Hercules.

At the time of writing, the company was paying a quarterly dividend with a robust 9.95% yield. But because of its foothold in the venture capital universe, Hercules also sees a level of capital appreciation from its warrant and equity-related investments that is very unusual for a BDC.

Over the last decade, the average annual return was more than 13.6%, along with steady growth in Hercules' overall portfolio assets. During that time, their total investment has enjoyed an average compound annual growth rate of more than 15% with net investment income growing roughly 16% annually.[2]

More than 90% of the Hercule's portfolio loans have variable interest rates. That means that if the government boosts interest rates, Hercules can too. This is a big advantage, and Hercules' management has speculated that even a modest boost in interest rates could increase the net interest annual income by several cents per share.

Of course, it's important to remember that BDCs face more volatility than conventional banks. But Hercules bridges the desire for solid, ongoing income returns with the long-term possibilities of some of the country's most innovative technology ventures. For many income investors, that's an exciting bridge to cross.

CHAPTER 6

HOW TO COLLECT MONTHLY RENT CHECKS
— WITHOUT OWNING A SINGLE PROPERTY

Own Thousands Of Properties Instead Of Just A Few

* * *

MOST PEOPLE HAVE CONSIDERED INVESTING IN REAL ESTATE AT some point. You've heard the stories — some regular folks buying a fixer-upper, putting in a little work, and lo and behold, 30 years later, it's worth $5 million!

You can open up any magazine or turn on any TV channel and hear these stories about real estate riches — the huge returns people get from investing in rental homes, apartment complexes or commercial real estate — but what we don't hear about is what a pain in the ass real estate can be.

Real estate is a tricky business. You need to own the property, maintain it, manage tenants... all of which is very expensive. Property ownership can open you up to a host of nightmare scenarios most people would want to avoid at all costs.

If you're handy, and you treat your property management as a job, it can work really well. I have a friend like this — he has a real estate portfolio, he manages all the properties himself, he leases them himself, he does a lot of the maintenance himself. That's his full-time job; it's all he does. Most people don't want to do that, especially if they're retired, and if you're younger, you probably already have a full-time job.

But there's no denying that real estate *is* an attractive investment, and fortunately for the income investor, now there's a way to invest in real estate without owning a single property.

A real estate investment trust (REIT) is a company that owns, operates or underwrites income-producing real estate, and different REITs specialize in different types of property (many of which we will explore in later sections). Similar in structure to mutual funds, REITs give you diverse exposure to real estate investments. Most importantly, they can provide a healthy stream of income, without the hassle, risk and volatility of having a small portfolio of private properties.

When you own a handful of properties privately, all your money is tied up in that handful of properties. I'd rather have my money distributed across 300 properties, where a team of seasoned real estate professionals are managing them.

I'm not a specialist in real estate, and don't have the clout on my own to really take advantage of the potential of large real estate investments, so I would rather have someone else handpick the investment properties, structure the investments to drive a healthy return, and oversee the property for the next 30 years or more.

A REIT can do that so much better than I could, and it creates a buffer from the risks associated with managing your own real estate, where you are personally on the hook for everything. If the roof is leaking on 1 of the 100 office buildings in the REIT's portfolio, it's only 1% of the buildings that have a problem, so it's fairly manageable.

But if you own a duplex and the roof is leaking, 50% of your investment has a problem, and it's going to cost you $20,000 personally to fix. That kind of cost can be catastrophic when you're trying to improve your income, and so investing in REITs protects you from that personal financial exposure. REITs are also run by experienced real estate investors — they know that each building will need a new roof every 20 years, and all the costs of maintenance and repairs have already been factored into their investments.

Additionally, REITs offer a critical form of diversification that most investors couldn't possibly manage on their own. REITs can own and manage a variety of property types: neighborhood shopping centers, health care facilities, apartments, single family homes, cell towers, warehouses, office buildings, hotels and more. Many REITs specialize in one particular type of property, such as shopping malls, self-storage facilities or large commercial spaces that they lease out to retailers such as Target and Walmart.

REITs also offer a form of liquidity that conventional property ownership could never compete with. Should you wish to sell your shares in a REIT, it's a matter of minutes before everything's done. That kind of quick transaction only exists in dreams if you want to sell an apartment complex or office space, and investing in a REIT is an affordable proposition for even the most modest investor.

Theoretically, you can buy a share of ownership in a REIT for $20 or $30, although some REITs per share price is significantly higher. Still, that pales in comparison with having to come up with a $100,000 deposit to buy a million-dollar apartment complex or office building. And that's not to mention the difference in fees between buying a property and buying shares in a REIT: commissions on the purchase or sale of a property can be as much as 6%. But the cost to buy shares in a REIT is typically just the commission — often less than $10, whether you are investing $1,000 or $100,000.

Geography can also be a factor in a REIT's portfolio diversification. Some invest throughout a country or even throughout the world. Others specialize in one particular region or even a single city or metropolitan area. Still others spread their holdings across different locations, a form of diversity that offers valuable protection. For instance, if the real estate market in Nashville is fluctuating, then cities with more stable conditions can counterbalance that and ensure that the investment remains stable overall.

REITs are sold to investors in much the same way as stocks and mutual funds. When you buy stock in a REIT, you earn a share of the income produced through the properties in which the REIT invests.

You can buy shares in REITs directly, through mutual funds or exchange traded funds (ETFs), and the income potential can be substantial. Most people invest in individual REITs, which trade just like stocks. There are also mutual funds and exchange traded funds that invest in multiple REITs (but the downside of investing in a fund that invests in REITs is that you pay more investment expenses — for example, you'll pay management fees to the fund, and the fund also passes on the REIT's expenses, so there's a second layer of fees there). Selecting 3 to 5 individual REITs is likely the best and most cost-effective approach.

By leasing space and collecting rent on the real estate it owns, a REIT generates income which is then paid out to shareholders in the form of dividends. REITs are legally obligated to distribute at least 90% of their taxable income to shareholders, which eliminates the possibility of the executive leadership deciding to reduce or eliminate dividends.

By law, REITs simply don't have that option. There are also ETFs that are made up exclusively of REITs. An ETF might own 50 REITs, which in turn might own 100 properties, so if you buy shares in that ETF, you own part of each of those REITs (and 50 x 100 = 5,000 properties). That means that with one purchase, you own a very diverse group of properties, all paying steady returns to shareholders. It's a highly effective and stable choice for the income investor.

Many stocks in the S&P 500 pay out dividends with an annual yield of less than 2%. Meanwhile, one of the biggest ETFs that owns real estate investment trusts is the **Vanguard Real Estate Investment Trust (Symbol:VNQ)**.

As of this writing, Vanguard is yielding nearly 4%, or double the yield of America's biggest blue-chip stocks. This disparity in the yield is largely explained by the fact that companies in the S&P 500 pay corporate taxes, whereas REITs avoid all taxes because they are obliged to pass through 90% of income to the shareholders.

REITs allow corporations to avoid tying up their capital in property ownership — whether it's a retail operation (such as Target, for example), a data center or a massive corporation, it's highly likely they lease the property from another owner. That's even the case with hotel chains.

Take Marriott, for example — even though their properties are branded as Marriott, they don't actually own the buildings. They're renting. Of course, the lease is a little different to the lease most people have on their apartment — often the lease spans decades, has interest rates attached to it and various conditions to retain the occupancy. But leasing still affords each company greater flexibility — if they need to move from a particular location or if their financials go sour, the company doesn't have to sell off any property (which is time-consuming and can delay access to critical funding). Leasing also is a plus for newer companies that would rather invest in product development or personnel.

Not only does that mean that there are ongoing opportunities for REITs to lease out the properties they own, and while many companies (and their related stocks) may suffer if sales dip, the rent on the property in which they do business still has to be paid. That's a level of reliability and certainty that many other investment options simply cannot offer.

Another major upside is that REITs are exempt from federal taxes, just like BDCs. Most corporations in the United States pay a 21% federal tax, but since REITs are required by law to distribute at least 90% of their taxable income out to their shareholders, the total amount of dividends to be distributed don't have that 21% taken off the top first.

EQUITY REITS VS MORTGAGE REITS

When you're doing your research about the different REITs, it's important to understand that there are few different ways REITs can handle their investments.

Equity REITs actually own their properties. They either borrow money from banks or issue bonds to get the cash they need up front, then source properties they think will offer healthy internal rates of return and cash flow, and then they will manage those properties internally or hire a property manager.

Meanwhile, mortgage REITs simply invest in the mortgages of properties. They don't actually *own* any properties.

For example, let's say you bought a house and your bank retains the loan. Often, your bank won't hold onto your loan for the 30-year duration of the mortgage — instead, they might sell that mortgage to a mortgage REIT. So your mortgage is owned by the REIT, not the bank that initially issued it. The mortgage REIT leverages their capital so that they can throw off lots of cash. These are a much more risky investment, but as a result, they're much higher yield.

And if that made you wonder about whether mortgage REITs had anything to do with the financial crash of 2008-2009, don't worry — mortgage REITs weren't the issue. Loose lending standards and incorrect ratings on risky mortgage loans (that were then packaged up together and misleadingly sold as safe investments) were to blame.

That said, mortgage REITs would have outsized risk in a credit crisis — unlike equity REITs that actually own the properties (which backs up the value of the investment), mortgage REITs are simply an investment in the ability of the borrowers to pay back the loans. So if a large portion of borrowers start to default, which is what happened in 2008, mortgage REITs would suffer.

One popular mortgage REIT ETF is the **iShares Mortgage Real Estate ETF (NYSE: REM)**. It currently has a yield of 8.95%, whereas Vanguard, the ETF that actually owns properties, is currently paying around 4%. So you can expect about twice as much yield from the mortgage REITs as you do from the equity REITs. This higher yield reflects the additional risk of mortgage REITs.

Part of this also depends on where we are in the economic cycle. If it's late in an economic cycle, and a downturn or recession seems likely, you're probably going to see more defaults on mortgages, and mortgage REITs could suffer as a result. But if we're in the earlier stages of the investment cycle, you would probably be less worried about that, and since you can collect up to twice as much yield, it might be more worth the risk if a crash doesn't look to be coming any time soon.

Again, this is why it's important to understand which type of REIT you are investing in, because your choice will largely be dictated by your appetite for risk and where we're at in the economic cycle.

CHAPTER 7

WHY UNCLE SAM IS THE PERFECT TENANT

The Federal Government's Go-To REIT

* * *

FINDING RELIABLE TENANTS WITH EQUALLY RELIABLE FUNDING can often be a challenge as a landlord. But there's one type of lease where that sort of uncertainty is largely eliminated, providing income investors with the sort of opportunity that's both attractive and stable.

Not only is the Federal Government of the United States the largest employer in the world, it's also the single largest office tenant in the country — and Uncle Sam pays his bills on time. Since 1998, the Government Services Administration (GSA) — the agency charged with providing facilities and other necessities to other areas of the federal government — has increased the amount of physical leased space by 24%. By contrast, inventory owned outright by the GSA has decreased by about 8% over that period.

That means that the GSA now leases far more than it owns. This is less expensive for taxpayers, and it also affords greater flexibility as offices and facilities can be transferred and rearranged much more readily. Given recent federal budget issues, it's reasonable to assume that the federal government will continue to grow its leased portfolio of assets, benefitting REITs including **Easterly Government Properties (Symbol: DEA).**

Easterly is a REIT with a particular focus on the acquisition, development and management of commercial properties that are leased to a variety of US government agencies and organizations. That covers a wide range of potential clients, from the Federal Bureau of Investigation (FBI) to the Coast Guard.

This niche creates a level of stability that is unusual, even in the steady world of equity REITs. For one thing, client financial solvency is basically a non-issue — it's pretty unlikely the CIA is going to skip out on paying their rent because they're going out of business.

Established in 2010, Easterly completed an initial public offering on the New York Stock Exchange, raising more than $200 million. Since its founding, Easterly has acquired 62 properties that takes in more than 5 million square feet. Roughly 97% of Easterly's real estate portfolio is leased to the US government.

While many of the properties are located in and around Washington D.C., others are situated in other parts of the country (for example, the government currently leases a 169,000-square-foot facility in Salt Lake City for use as an FBI field office.)

Easterly deals exclusively with the federal government, which allows them to avoid working with state and local government entities which are not backed by the full faith and credit of the United States government (the GSA has never financially defaulted on a lease throughout its history.) And rather than leasing to *all* federal government entities, they focus on agencies with "enduring missions" — the groups whose activity is predictable and highly likely to remain in place. These include offices like the Federal Bureau of Investigation, Immigration and Customs Enforcement, the Department of Agriculture and so on. Most of those agencies prohibit telecommuting, which means they are always going to need a physical space to accommodate their personnel.

Not only does Easterly lease to a broad range of government offices and agencies, the company owns an equally diverse range of facilities. Over 70% of the company's holdings are office space, with the remaining properties largely made up of laboratories (9%), Veterans Administration outpatient locations (10%) and courthouses and related offices (5%). The following map shows the firm's geographic diversification.

Source: https://easterlyreit.com/properties/

To ensure an investment is going to be appropriate and profitable, Easterly uses a comprehensive underwriting process. Prior to purchasing any building, the company examines the physical condition of the property, and also assesses it for potential client use as well. Finally, they consider the property's adaptability and ease of alteration to make it suitable for use by specific government offices and agencies.

The company's emphasis on stability is also reflected in its lease terms. Easterly has long-term initial lease structures of up to 20 years, with renewal terms that are often as long as 10 years, and its average lease is 13.5 years.

Additionally, the company leverages an operating expense increase structure based on the Consumer Price Index (CPI). That means that annual rent increases are tied to the CPI, which ensures that rent payments stay in step with inflation. To top things off, the GSA generally pays all property tax increases.

These factors contribute to a highly stable income source. Easterly is currently paying a yield of 5.2%, far more attractive than many big-name stocks. The company's quarterly dividend has increased 136% since 2015. However, the increases in recent years have been very modest.

Meanwhile, stock price appreciation has been minimal since the company went public. While there may be higher yielding REITs, this is a top choice for people looking for safe and steady income.

The stability and solvency of Easterly's work with the federal government makes this a solid pick for any income investor — particularly those looking for a trusted source of income in any type of economy.

CHAPTER 8

HOW TO INVEST IN WARREN BUFFETT'S REIT OF CHOICE

The Investment Mogul's Only REIT Is Open For Investment

* * *

IN MID-2017, WARREN BUFFETT AND BERKSHIRE HATHAWAY invested $377 million in **STORE Capital (NYSE: STOR)**, a retail REIT. That investment represented nearly 10% of STORE's outstanding shares, which means it was a very significant play from Berkshire Hathaway, *and* STORE is the only REIT in their iconic portfolio.

And it's not just a significant play for Berkshire Hathaway — it's a significant play for income investors, too. Recently STORE's dividend was a substantial 4.3%, double that of the average S&P 500 company, and there is still plenty of room for the company to expand. STORE estimates the market for properties suitable for its portfolio (over 1.9 million additional properties) to have a market value of $3 trillion.

Working backwards from their investment thesis — that they want to buy great companies at a fair price, to be held forever — we have to assume Berkshire Hathaway believes in the future of physical retail. STORE is an acronym for Single Tenant Operational Real Estate, and at the time of writing, the company's portfolio had investments in 2,334 property locations, with an estimated overall value of $6.7 billion. Here's a map showing those locations:

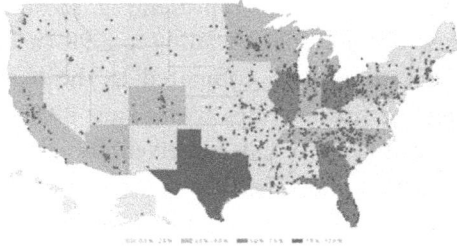

Source: STORE Capital

To be absolutely specific, STORE is a net-lease REIT. That means that all tenants must cover part or all of the taxes, fees and maintenance costs for the property, in addition to the rent. Compared to traditional commercial real estate, where the landlord picks up those variable expenses, this is an unusual arrangement and is obviously a powerful way for STORE to decrease their costs on each property.

Typically, net leases carry long initial terms — normally 15 years of more — with annual rent increases, or escalators, built into the agreement. In STORE's case, the average lease has roughly 14 years left on its term with average annual rent increases on existing leases of 1.8%. Additionally, most of these leases also have a consumer price index component — if the CPI rises, so does the rent.

All these factors have allowed STORE to build a predictable and growing income, and to diversify extensively. In fact, referring to STORE as a retail-focused REIT is a bit reductive, since the company goes well beyond standard retail operations.

Their tenants operate across a wide variety of industries within the service, retail and manufacturing sectors, with a particular concentration on restaurants, furniture stores, early childhood education, movie theaters and health clubs — all operations that are impossible to deliver online. Overall, more than 440 tenants representing more than 100 industries lease STORE space, leading to a 99.7% occupancy rate. That's incredibly high compared to the overall retail industry, where occupancy rates average just 89.8%.[1]

STORE's approach to the perceived threat to physical retail from Amazon and other e-commerce marketplaces is another attractive aspect — they focus on leasing to large, established and financially sound companies which are in a good position to fend off e-commerce disruption. They have taken several important steps to offset the threat, and they are highly selective in choosing companies to whom they will lease.

For one thing, the REIT evaluates tenants on a unit-level basis, which cuts down on the possibility of bankruptcy and unanticipated vacancies. They make a practice of acquiring properties at prices below their replacement cost, and since no single tenant is responsible for more than 3% of the REIT's revenue, the effect of one tenant going under would be minimal to the health of the overall portfolio.

This careful approach to acquiring new properties and reliable tenants has produced strong funds from operations (FFO) and a steadily growing dividend which seems likely to continue on its upward trajectory.

CHAPTER 9

EARN REAL ESTATE RICHES WITH AGING AMERICA

Senior Communities Promise Major Returns

* * *

WHILE THERE ARE VERY FEW SURE THINGS IN LIFE, TIME passing us by is one of them. In America, more and more of us are getting old. According to the World Bank, the life expectancy of the average American is now just under 79 years, and the Census Bureau projects that people over

65 will shortly comprise 20% of the U.S. population. Although greater life expectancy can be tied to healthier habits and vastly improved medical technology, aging inevitably means that we need greater ongoing medical attention and long-term care.

Senior living communities are an ideal solution to these problems, and we're seeing a boom in REIT interest in this area, which is the focus of two very successful healthcare REITs — Welltower and HealthCare Realty Trust.

Welltower (NYSE: WELL) focuses on investing in senior housing, long-term care and post-acute care properties, along with outpatient medical facilities. Their investments are located throughout the United States, and in several foreign countries. As of this writing, Welltower's portfolio consists of 1,502 healthcare properties. With some 321,000 residents, roughly two-thirds of the company's income comes from senior housing properties, with outpatient medical facilities (approximately 16%) and long-term and post-care facilities (about 10%) accounting for the remainder.

Given how demographics are changing in the US, the number of senior citizens requiring housing will only go up. The number of people over 85 is expected to increase at a much faster rate than the number of people aged 25 to 34. That growth will also run parallel to the number of people suffering from dementia, which is currently forecast to double every 20 years. It's terrible to see such a debilitating disease become so prevalent, but with companies like Welltower in place, there will at least be a good standard of care and accommodation in place for this population.

Welltower's outpatient locations see more than 15 million patients every year. That establishes a multi- pronged approach to care — housing facilities for those who need some form of assisted living, as well as outpatient medical treatment to address the health needs of patients of all ages.

Overall, their holdings makes Welltower the fifth largest real estate company in the US by enterprise value. The company is currently paying a 5.6% dividend, and they boast a 240% total return for the past decade, which beats the pants off the large cap S&P 500 index.

Welltower has been consistent in maintaining its dividend payouts, even while other REITs have cut or eliminated dividends. In fact, over the last decade the dividend has been increased by 28%. They've been able to do this thanks to a conservative operating philosophy, specifically designed to shield investors from market downturns with light debt and a cash heavy position.

Another option for income investors in the medical facility field is **Healthcare Realty Trust (NYSE: HR)**. Like Welltower, Healthcare Realty's focus is on medical-related properties but with a slightly different angle — instead of residential properties, HR's target is medical office buildings.

The company currently owns 201 properties, taking in 14.9 million square feet of space. The majority of properties are multi-tenant facilities located throughout the United States, mostly in large cities with healthy economies and growing populations. Currently, HR's most important market is Dallas, which accounts for 15.9% of their total investments. Other major cities with significant HR investments include Seattle, Charlotte, Denver and Los Angeles.

The company has been particularly aggressive in acquiring new properties in recent years, emphasizing its core target of medical facilities and getting rid of other kinds of properties.

This is geared to long-term stability and growth in a single market — the more niche their focus, the better able they will be to spot good deals and maintain great facilities. For instance, HR owns the University of Maryland Medical Center, which it leases to the school, and it has similar arrangements at the University of Colorado and Indiana University. This allows major teaching and care programs to emphasize their own core missions, while leaving any concerns about sourcing and maintaining suitable facilities up to HR.

The company has also boosted its acquisition of medical facilities with the development of satellite properties, including urgent care locations, cancer treatment offices, outpatient surgeries, imaging offices and other facilities with specific types of medical care. Over the last 20 years, Healthcare Realty has developed more than 4 million square feet of outpatient medical facilities, with an investment of over $1 billion.

HR's dividend yield is a bit less than that of Welltower, currently around 4%. But, like Welltower, the company is well-positioned to leverage growth in the healthcare industry. Its focus is not quite as specific as Welltower's particular emphasis on care for the growing senior citizen population, but with a broad mandate in health care in an aging environment, HR is also a solid bet for future income potential.

CHAPTER 10

COLLECTING CASH ON THE TOLL ROAD OF THE INTERNET

Connecting The World Means Breakthrough Profits For Companies — And You

* * *

IMAGINE IF YOU COULD GET PAID EVERY TIME YOU WATCHED A movie on Netflix or streamed an album on Spotify. Well, the dream is real, and you can finally make cash sitting on the couch, watching your favorite shows.

Cloud technology (multiple computers linked together via the Internet, to distribute the storage of data across space that's otherwise not being used), allows online entertainment companies to stream content instantly. Data storage is a huge opportunity for the income investor that understands just how much growth is still to happen online.

This map shows how the entire world is interconnected. The companies that provide connectivity — and allow for access to information — can earn huge profits:

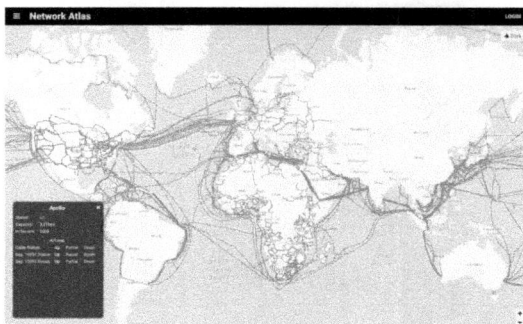

Source: https://www.pressrelease.com/news/network-atlas-launches-map-of-global-internet-infrastructure-133783

The folks that own the cloud technology charge their clients a small fee every time a user watches a video, reads an article, or downloads an app. You can think of this service like the toll road of the Internet — you get a great service, but you have to pay to play. While most REITs focus on traditional physical real estate, in the online economy, the only real estate that matters is data storage. One REIT has locked in on investing in the cloud, and you can sit there in the toll booth with them, collecting a percentage of the fees every time a user passes through.

Digital Realty Trust (NYSE: DLR) is a REIT that provides IT infrastructure and data centers to its clients. If a business needs IT to support cloud-based activities (whether they are a regional insurance firm or an entertainment giant like Netflix), Digital Realty can provide the infrastructure they need.

That includes real estate, buildings and facilities for operations like cloud services and telecom providers. They can also handle corporate IT activities like networking, cloud storage, digital media, colocation, and connected campus, security and compliance programs.

As of this writing, the company manages 203 data centers in 12 countries, covering 32 metropolitan areas and 32 million rentable square feet. Those facilities provide Internet connectivity for high-end tech companies, investment banks and other large corporate clients (including IBM, Century-Link, AT&T, Verizon, Tata Communications, JP Morgan Chase and VISA).

It seems likely that the data facility requirements of these companies, and others like them, will only increase in the future, offering Digital Realty and other similar companies ripe opportunities for continued growth as well.

Not only is Digital Realty in a new part of the REIT industry, it also has a strong foothold in an area that's expected to grow substantially in the years ahead. The global data center transformation market is expected to nearly double from $6.45 billion in 2018 to $12 billion by 2023, for a compound annual growth rate of more than 13%.

That's a direct result of growth in overall data center traffic, which is projected to double every two years. The following table will give you a sense of just how quickly Internet usage has increased in the last 30 years or so, and shows how incredibly quickly it is still growing:

Table 1. The Cisco VNI Forecast: Historical Internet Context

Year	Global Internet Traffic
1992	100 GB per hour
1997	100 GB per hour
2002	100 GB per hour
2007	100 GB per hour
2017	100 GB per hour
2022	100 GB per hour

Source: Cisco VNI, 2018

That growth is also likely to continue expanding. Increased use of the Internet of Things (like voice-activated devices) and artificial intelligence, data generated by self-driving cars and increased online activity will continue to put pressure on these facilities to expand. Digital Realty's occupancy rate is currently at about 90%, and that's only going to increase too.

Another advantage is the specificity required for data center locations — not just any shed will do. Data centers are designed to provide a controlled environment for servers and network equipment, and the buildings house enormous server farms and networking equipment to enable cloud computing. These facilities also require highly reliable and secure environments for redundancy backup systems that protect the cooling, mechanical and electrical processes that prevent data loss.

Digital Realty has aggressively grown into this environment with key acquisitions and other forms of expansion. In September 2017, the company announced the completion of an all-stock merger with DuPont Fabros with an enterprise value of about $7.8 billion. That move enhanced the company's portfolio in the top US data-center metro areas across Northern Virginia, Chicago and Silicon Valley. Digital Realty has also opened its third data center in Toronto, further expanding the company's presence in the fourth largest city in North America (and the commerce capital of Canada).

In addition to providing suitable locations, Digital Realty also operates the data centers. It's a major value-add for clients, who need safe, reliable data center space where they can access state of the art facilities — without the financial burden of having to buy the space outright or worry about technical operational issues.

That puts Digital Realty in a similar position to many other REITs — focusing on a core activity while providing attractive returns to its investors. As is the case with all REITs, Digital Realty is required by law to pay out at least 90% of its taxable income to investors, which currently translates to a 3.5% yield.

The dividend has continued to grow, and the stock price has continued to rise as well: since the company started paying dividends in 2013, it's increased 38%, and they have increased the payments every year since then.[1]

The management at DR has been conservative recently as we approach the end of the economic cycle, trimming dividends in order to boost its asset base. By the end of 2018, DR had a market capitalization of more than $25 billion, making it the seventh largest publicly traded REIT in the United States.

Another advantage in DR's model is that unlike other forms of commercial property leases, data centers generally offer fairly short-term leases. Given the high rate of change in the data industry and companies' needs to adjust accordingly, a data center lease will usually be no more than 5 years.

While this seems very short compared to the typical lease length for other REITs, it makes DR much more agile. For instance, if the price of acquiring new properties goes up, the company is better positioned to raise its lease rates to offset the additional expense. The same holds true with bandwidth costs; if prices jump, they can readily pass on the expense to customers.

Of course, there's always a downside to consider, and for DR that comes in the form of competition from players outside the REIT world. While Digital Realty has developed state-of-the-art technology to support their clients, each of those clients certainly has the financial means to build their own data centers (particularly those large-scale players, such as Google, Microsoft, and Amazon, whose company Amazon

Web Services has one of the largest data center operations in the world).

However, many other large companies have recently decided against building their own data centers due to the cost of construction and other drawbacks, even to the point of selling off existing facilities.

Overall, Digital Realty is a solid company with a proven track record of providing shareholders with a steady stream of income. They are in an industry that's unlikely to go away, and Digital Realty and their management is doing a great job managing their growth over the long term.

CHAPTER 11

"HOW LONG ARE YOU STAYING?"

The A-Z On Hotel REITs

* * *

LIKE HEALTHCARE, RESIDENTIAL AND GOVERNMENT PROPERTY, hospitality and travel are also attractive investment industries that are completely out of each for most individual investors. According to the US Travel Association, domestic travel increased 1.9% from 2017 to a total of 2.29 billion personal trips in 2018. Breaking that down a bit further, domestic leisure travel increased 7.1% in 2018 to 1.82 billion individual trips. Domestic business travel rose 1.6% from 2017 to 463 million trips.[1]

The economic impact of those numbers is enormous. In 2018, domestic travelers alone spent $933 billion in the U.S. (an increase of 5.8% from 2017). That financial outlay directly supported 7.7 million jobs and generated $147 billion in tax revenues for federal, state and local governments. Hotel companies profit accordingly, no matter if it's Hilton, Westin or any number of other recognizable names.

As of this writing, **Hilton Hotels (HLT)** is paying a dividend with a 1.1% yield — not exactly spectacular. But it's important to recognize that Hilton, like many other large hotel chains, doesn't actually own many of the properties that bear its name. Instead, they prefer to lease properties, an arrangement which gives them greater financial and logistical flexibility. That's why, if you stay at a particular hotel in a particular city one year, it's possible that on your next visit, that very same property will sport a different name.

Chatham Lodging Trust (NYSE: CLDT) is a REIT specializing in hotels, and there are some particular advantages to this type of portfolio.

Therein lies the opportunity of a REIT such as Chatham Lodging Trust. In mid-2019, Chatham was paying a very healthy 7.2% dividend yield — more than 6 times that offered by Hilton. Although Chatham's portfolio includes a number of well-known hotel brands (Courtyard Marriott, Hilton Gardens and others), the REIT is completely detached from the mechanics of operating profitable hotels. Instead, they're focused on leasing out hotel space, and ultimately, returning capital to shareholders — what every investor should look for in any company.

And according to a press release from Chatham, they have been very successful at sourcing this available space. The company owns interests in 135 hotels, totaling 18,592 rooms and suites, comprised of 40 properties it wholly owns with an aggregate of 6,092 rooms and suites in 15 states (and the District of Columbia). It also holds a minority investment in 2 joint ventures that own 95 hotels with an aggregate of 12,500 rooms and suites.[2]

Another Chatham advantage is the varied lease arrangements the company maintains with its tenants. Some leases extend out as far as 2045, while other expire in just a few years. That affords long-term security, balanced with the flexibility and liquidity of shorter contracts.

The company has also proactively addressed a potential downside to long-term contracts by incorporating scheduled rent increases into a number of their agreements. For instance, the lease agreement for a property in Pennsylvania incorporates minimum annual rent increases of 2.5%, and rent can be adjusted to increase if the hotel exceeds 85% occupancy.

Chatham's recent profitability shows a thoughtful, strategic outlook to new acquisitions: they are focused on acquiring hotel properties in markets that have strong demand and where they expect growth to outpace supply. For instance, the company spent $21 million to buy the 96-room Residence Inn Charleston Summerville, S.C., under construction at the time.

The location is beautiful, but more importantly, the hotel is adjacent to the 96-room Courtyard by Marriott that Chatham already owns. These hotels are located in Nexton, a growing, mixed-use community in the heart of a rapidly expanding area just outside of Charleston, and the hotels will be the closest accommodations to Volvo's second planned American plant, guaranteeing a steady flow of occupancy and partnership opportunities.

All this has added up to solid, steady growth. Company revenue has increased at a double-digit rate for the past several years. Chatham's earnings before interest, tax, depreciation and amortization margin (EBITDA) are also among the best in the industry, which shows a healthy day- to-day operational profitability. Chatham's dividend has also increased steadily over the past several years, and they've grown without unnecessary debt levels. And as a final plus for investors looking for particularly consistent income sources, Chatham distributes its dividends every month instead of quarterly.

Now, no investment or industry is completely bulletproof, and Chatham is no exception. Even though its diverse holdings are more robust than investments in individual properties, Chatham's financial performance is still impacted by the economy. If fewer people are traveling, it's going to show up, one way or another, in the company's financials. Interest rates are also a bit more likely to affect hotel REITs than other types of investments — any significant increase in the cost of borrowing will affect Chatham's property acquisition and renovation activities.

Nonetheless, Chatham ticks all the boxes for a profitable REIT investment — it's diversified, it has an attractive yield and is efficiently operated by management with a proven track record of success.

CHAPTER 12

INVESTMENT INCOME THAT'S 100% EXEMPT FROM ALL FEDERAL INCOME TAXES

Take Advantage of America's Energy With Master Limited Partnerships

* * *

New sources of energy are emerging as important new parts of the economy, but it's going to take a long time for the US to shift away from using oil and gas, and you stand to make a very tidy income in the meantime from the existing energy sector.

Energy has been a hot-button issue for as long as many of us can remember — starting with the 'energy crisis' of the 1970s with its memories of endless lines at gas station pumps. But, as it turns out, that crisis wasn't all bad news and consumer frustration. One of the best income investment vehicles we have available today comes from that time — master limited partnerships, or MLPs.

MLPs were created in 1981 by President Reagan, partially as a response to the challenges the United States was facing with regard to energy, including soaring prices and unreliable supplies. The goal was to encourage investment in US energy infrastructure, so the President gave these MLPs a tax break, and allowed them to pay nothing in corporate taxes. Similar to REITs, MLPs were designed as publicly traded partnerships to raise capital from individual investors, to promote the development of natural energy resources, associated infrastructure and the broader goal of energy independence. (MLPs have since expanded into a diverse array of industries.)

In spite of the fact that we currently have the largest supply of renewable energy in the United States that we've ever had, oil production is also at an all-time high. While we're likely to see a gradual shift towards more renewable use, it's a very long time before renewables will replace oil and gas. Both of those are at full production — in the 1990s and early 2000s, oil production shrunk in the US, but we've seen it bounce back to the levels we were seeing in the 1970s.

The following chart shows that US crude oil production has recently reached all-time record highs. This is largely due to technology advancements — including fracking — that have allowed America to enjoy an energy renaissance in the last decade.

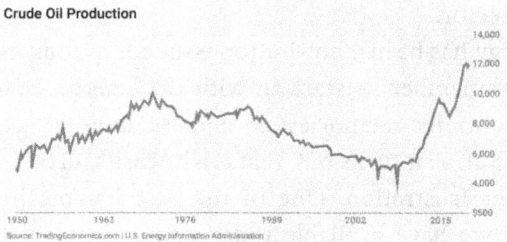

Crude Oil Production

While reducing non-renewable energy sources is going to be good for humanity, good for the planet (and good for the economy as well), the reality is that the move away from oil and gas is going to be a lengthy process that takes many decades.

Investors tend to focus on what's happening in the near-term, and while the long-term stuff can be exciting, those big ideas are often a decade or more away. But most of us are focused on what's happening in the next few months, what's happening this year, *maybe* what's happening next year, especially when we're thinking about how to increase our income investments.

It used to be that people thought we were running out of oil and gas. And in 2008-2009, we started hearing we had reached 'peak oil' — the idea that we had reached the upper limit of what we would be able to extract from the ground.

But with new technology, including fracking, we've discovered so much oil and gas within our own borders that America's recoverable oil reserves are larger than Saudi Arabia's. Estimates suggest that the country has 310 billion barrels of recoverable oil. That's equal to 79 years of US production at current levels — more good news for companies providing infrastructure and supply services to support that production. In the next decade, oil is going to remain a huge source of energy and a necessity for our society and economy.

Oil and gas prices fluctuate considerably, and when we see a lot of volatility, it can really hurt the companies that are pulling those resources out of the ground. One of the reasons MLPs are such a great investment is that they are largely protected from that volatility. They're not the ones doing the actual drilling for oil and gas — they are simply providing services and infrastructure to the mining industry. It's a bit like what happened during the gold rush in California — a few people struck gold and got rich, but the people who really made a lot of money were folks like Levi Strauss, who was selling jeans to everyone out there working. MLPs are a lot like Mr. Strauss, providing something that's critical to get the job done.

We are seeing a resurgence in the prevalence of US-sourced oil and natural gas — it's booming all over the country, from Western Pennsylvania to Arkansas, from North Dakota to Texas. Oil and gas companies are drilling up resources and then need to get the material to refineries, where it can be refined into useful products. That's where MLPs come in. They take the thick, sludgy crude oil that's pumped up out of the ground and move it to where it can be refined into the fine, slick product that's going to turn into gasoline to go into your car or gas to heat your home.

You can think of MLPS as the patrons of America's energy renaissance, and without these companies, the industry wouldn't exist. The alternative, where pipelines don't exist, is to put crude oil in tanker cars to be transported by train across the country, which is extremely dangerous. There have been various instances where a train carrying crude oil goes off the rails and explodes (sometimes, tragically, killing dozens of people, as happened in Lac-Mégantic disaster in Canada in 2013[1]).

Crude oil is highly flammable and shouldn't be transported in such a volatile way — the pipelines are a much safer, much more reliable and efficient system. They are built underground and the oil just flows all day, every day, at a steady pace, without disrupting anything or endangering anyone, and most people don't even know they exist. They're a necessity, and a massive improvement on rail transport, which means that they're also a good bet for producing regular, low-risk income.

MLPs are also not exposed to world events like oil and gas companies are. They're not affected by tariffs or trade wars, they're not affected by fluctuations in commodity pricing, and they're not affected by actual conflicts either. These are US-based and US-focused companies, and so while they might refine products to export to other markets, their business is primarily domestic — all the pipes and refineries are built into the ground within the country's borders. And these companies are vast. **Energy Transfer (NYSE: ET)**, one of the major MLPs operating today, has around 86,000 miles of pipeline across dozens of projects. This also ensures continuing stability for the investment — even if something happened to one of them, or a particular project failed, the risk is very distributed and so any single problem would be very unlikely to cause flow-on effects to the investors.

When you're looking into buying into an MLP, the key is to choose those that are responsibly managed. Some MLPs are highly leveraged, and those are usually smaller, up-and-coming concerns. Large companies, including MLPs, tend to be better managed and more conservative in their approach, which is what you're going to care about if you're counting on them to make regular income payments to you. Focusing on the larger ones leads you to owning ones that will be safer and more secure.

There are several MLPs that are good options for income investors looking to capitalize on this thriving industry. Energy Transfer, mentioned earlier, is based in Dallas, Texas, and on top of its extensive network of natural gas and crude pipelines, it also maintains storage facilities and other infrastructure in 38 states. This map shows the company's impressive operations and nation-wide reach:

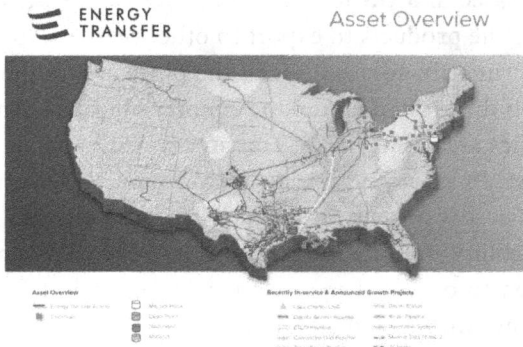

Source: https://www.energytransfer.com/

Similar to REITs, MLPs such as Energy Transfer are designed to pass as much income as possible through to investors. And, like REITs, ET returns more than 90% of its income to investors, making it completely exempt from federal income taxes. And that pass through has been exceedingly generous. As of this writing, ET was yielding 8.2% — that's 4 times greater than the average S & P 500 stock. ET recently merged with another MLP, which reduced its yield a little — prior to the merger it had been yielding around 10%, so it's reasonable to expect that the yield might climb again after things settle down again after this change.

Like all investments, MLPs occasionally come in for some bad press. One example is the 2017 protests against ET, the parent company of Dakota Access (the company responsible for developing the controversial Dakota Access Pipeline that runs through the Midwestern United States). When it commenced operations in 2017, the pipeline became the focus of protests and lawsuits seeking to shut it down.

Environmental and social concerns have been a persistent part of the news cycle around the project and this is likely to happen for any major new developments by MLPs.

However, this is a 'headline risk' — not an investment risk. Bad press passes: the investment itself has not really suffered from this scrutiny, as negative headlines don't have any impact on the actual value of the investment. MLPs are also inextricably linked to a volatile industry.

They are not directly involved in drilling for gas or oil, nor the geological activities and exploration that precede drilling, but their clients are. If oil prices drop, companies that do oil exploration and production obviously suffer, and will often slow down their projects. That, in turn, impacts the industry support sectors — there's less oil to be transported, which translates to less need for new or existing transport infrastructure. That can lead those producers to renegotiate transportation costs, cutting into the income of pipeline operators.

Debt can also be an issue. Building new pipelines is extremely expensive, and ET and most other MLPs manage a significant level of ongoing debt. However, the industry continues to thrive, and according to Reuters in 2019, "the Dallas-based pipeline operator has almost completed a 120,000 bpd expansion of its Permian Express System, a joint venture with Exxon Mobil Corp, with the system's full capacity coming into service by the end of the third quarter of 2019."[2]

For investors who want a greater level of portfolio diversity than ET offers, there are also ETFs made up of MLPs. The **Alerian MLP Exchange (NYSE: AMLP)** currently has a portfolio of 27 holdings, all of which are focused on energy. The fund is currently yielding nearly 5% and gives investors access to a broad range of infrastructure companies in the energy sector.

CHAPTER 13

WANT BLUE CHIP STOCKS AT DISCOUNT PRICES?

Choose The Dogs Of The Dow

* * *

WHEN YOU'RE CHOOSING STOCKS TO BUY FOR YOUR PORTFOLIO, it's usually best to keep it simple. Buying shares of great companies isn't rocket science, and it doesn't need to take up tons of your time or energy. The goal here is to create income — without it turning into another job.

That's why I think you'll love this strategy. It doesn't require a lot of heavy lifting, you only have to look at it once a year, and it ensures you pick stocks that are high quality and high return.

The Dogs of the Dow is a straightforward and profitable income investment strategy. It's the ideal formula for people who want reliable quarterly payments — without spending hours every week planning, executing and monitoring a complex investment plan.

Each year, you simply buy the 10 stocks within the Dow Jones Industrial Average with the highest dividend yield.

This strategy was popularized by Michael O'Higgins in his book, *Beating the Dow*. While the strategy can be implemented at any time of year, most people buy the 10 Dogs of the Dow stocks on the first day of the year. From there, it's just a matter of holding and repeating the process annually at year's end, with no need to rebalance or reconfigure at any other time during the year. At the end of the next year, you adjust your portfolio to account for any changes in those top 10 yielding stocks.

Between 1999 and 2017, the Dogs of the Dow easily beat the benchmark Dow Jones Industrials:

Source: https://seekingalpha.com/article/4038693-
make-dogs-dow-howl

The Dow Jones is one of the oldest indexes in the world, and lists just 30 companies. By buying the third that have the highest yield, you're investing in the companies that are going to pay you the most income, *and* you're likely to see some capital appreciation. There's a wide range of yields on the index but the average is around 2%. Meanwhile, the Dogs of the Dow deliver 50% to 100% more than the typical stock in the Dow Jones, often yielding between 3% and 6%.

The reason the Dogs of the Dow have a higher yield is because often they've underperformed market expectations in the past year, and their stock price has fallen. Yield and price work inversely with each other: when the stock price goes down, the yield goes up (assuming the dividend payments remain constant). For example, let's say a stock has a dividend of 2%, and that one day something happens that causes the company's stock price to drop by 50%. If the company doesn't change the dividend they pay out, the dividend as a percentage will increase from 2% to 4%.

But to be clear, investing in the Dogs doesn't mean you're speculating on companies on the brink of failure. In fact, it's the opposite — all of the companies in the Dow Jones Industrials are massive, stable companies that have consistently delivered outstanding results. The Dogs of the Dow simply have the lowest performance of the year within this high-achieving index. And that means they can pay out higher yields and may be ripe for a rebound in the coming year. This is a great opportunity, because individual investors can afford to buy more stock in high quality companies and to enjoy high yields with companies that are currently underpriced.

When December 31st rolls around again, you reallocate your portfolio, based on how those companies have moved around in the index. You look at the 30 Dow stocks again, and find the 10 that have the highest yield (some will probably be the same as the previous year, and some will be new). You keep the ones that you already have, sell those that are no longer on the list of 10, and buy up their replacements.

The market has a cycle where companies go in and out of favor with investors, based on various factors, from performance to public perception. The same is true of the Dogs of the Dow — they are last year's least popular companies, so there is certainly a contrarian approach here.

Instead of investing in the things that are really popular right now, you invest in the things that are out of favor, safe in the knowledge that there's not much turnover on the Dow Jones. These are all safe and stable companies, many of which have been in business for over 50 years, so while we're buying the ones that are less popular today, that doesn't mean they're not a great investment. Here's the list of the 2019 Dogs of the Dow, their Dow Jones ticker symbols, and their yields:

- IBM (**IBM**): 5.5%
- ExxonMobil (**XOM**): 4.8%
- Verizon (**VZ**): 4.3%
- Chevron (**CVX**): 4.1%
- Pfizer (**PFE**): 3.3%
- Coca-Cola (**KO**): 3.3%
- JP Chase Morgan (**JPM**): 3.3%
- Proctor & Gamble (**PG**): 3.1%
- Cisco Systems (**CSCO**): 3%
- Merck (**MRK**): 2.9%

Currently, the Dogs are yielding roughly 4% on average — around double the S&P 500 with a dividend yield below 2%. This strategy is also very cost efficient, given its core principle of buy and hold. Turnover among the Dogs of the Dow is low (the list averages about two changes per year), which means that you're not spending much on commissions to buy and sell your shares.

Of course, everything comes down to investment performance. Overall, as a long-term strategy, the Dogs perform well against the rest of the market. 2017 was a rough year for the Dogs, returning 19% versus 25% for the Dow Jones as a whole, although dividend income was slightly greater for the Dogs. But there have been periods when the Dogs have consistently beaten competing benchmarks — between 2010 and 2017, the Dogs produced outsized returns in 6 of the 7 years. Additionally, from 1992 to 2011, the Dogs were up an average of 10.8% versus the S & P 500's 9.6%.

While that difference may only be a percentage point or so, even that slight disparity can add up to significant profit over time (keeping in mind the plan to buy the Dogs and hold them for the long haul).

There are also options available for investors interested in a more targeted strategy. A similar approach, known as the Small Dogs of Dow (fondly known as 'the puppies'), involves investing in just 5 companies found on the 10-company Dogs list. You choose the 5 stocks with the lowest share prices, in order to capitalize on potential stock price appreciation as much as possible.

Between 2008 and 2018, the Small Dogs of the Dow earned a 15.9% annualized return. That was slightly better than the standard Dogs of the Dow and 2.3% ahead of the Dow Jones Industrials.[1]

Despite all the advantages, some analysts have criticized the Dogs of the Dow strategy for being too simple (which, depending on your worldview, might be because it makes their 'expertise' obsolete), and that investors should weigh their commitment based on stock price and yield rather than investing the same amount in all 10 stocks.

Others have suggested that a high yield can mean that a stock's price is about to drop instead of indicating an attractive, undervalued holding, and that the strategy fails to take this possibility into account.

No investment strategy is perfect, and as Warren Buffett reminds us, no one can predict what the market is going to do, but the Dogs of the Dow is a proven means of generating a solid income investing portfolio that's easily accessible for individuals.

Simplicity is the key to this strategy. Too often, people make investing unnecessarily complicated, believing that complexity equals profits. But that's just not true. Sometimes success means making things so simple that you can't help but succeed.

This why the Dogs and Small Dogs have become so popular among buy-and-hold investors. In a world of complex trading strategies, this straightforward approach allows you to invest in solid companies with high yield and good growth potential — an effective formula for earning more and paying less for any investment you choose to make.

CHAPTER 14

AMERICA'S CROWN JEWELS: COMPANIES WHO HAVE PAID INVESTORS FOR UP TO 25 YEARS IN A ROW

Elite Stocks With Astonishing Track Records

* * *

DIVIDEND ACHIEVERS AND ARISTOCRATS ARE POWERFUL AND profitable choices for the individual income investor. As we discussed in the earlier section on dividend growth, some companies raise their dividends religiously every year. Dividend achievers are companies that have raised their dividends for at least 10 consecutive years, and dividend aristocrats are companies that have raised them for at least 25 consecutive years. These companies are the jewels in our economy.

Among America's 500 largest and most respected brands, 89% don't meet the criteria to be part of this elite group. While many companies pay dividends, that alone is not enough to reach this status. To qualify, companies have to increase their payments every single year — even in years when things are terrible. Many of the companies on these lists increased their dividends during the Great Depression, during the Dot Com bust of the 1990s, and even during the economic craziness after the 9/11 terrorist attacks. These companies are among the most exclusive, stable and profitable companies in the world.

There's so much prestige in retaining a place on these lists, that there's even less variability in the Achiever and Aristocrat lists than the 10 highest-yielding companies of the Dogs of the Dow. In my view, if you want to know which companies are likely to continue raising their dividends, focus on the companies that have a history of doing just that.

Both the Dividend Achievers and Dividend Aristocrats are groups of companies that are listed on the New York Stock Exchange and NASDAQ, and both must meet specific criteria to be included. The list of Achievers is made up of 264 stocks with over 10 consecutive years of dividend increases, while there are just 57 Aristocrats: S&P 500 stocks with over 25 consecutive years of dividend increases. Both lists have minimum size and liquidity requirements, which makes both groups decidedly elite — the Aristocrats account for just 10% of the companies listed on the S&P 500.

Both lists include iconic companies you've probably heard of, like ExxonMobil, Colgate-Palmolive, Johnson & Johnson, but both lists also feature dozens of companies that aren't household names (such as AbbVie, a pharmaceutical research company, Leggett & Platt, an engineering manufacturer, and Cardinal Health, a healthcare logistics company). This highlights the fact that great investments aren't always where you expect to find them — often, the most famous companies aren't going to pay you the best dividends.

Every company included on these lists has actively prioritized their commitment to shareholders, and have done so amid years of upheaval and change which have prompted other companies to cut or even eliminate dividends completely. Dividend growth is so important because it shows a commitment to shareholders above all else. These companies recognize that their shareholders deserve more income, every single year, and that this is the company's first priority.

All income investors should be focused on the actual amount of income they receive from their investment (remember what my colleague Steve tells me: "Income investing IS investing. Everything else is simply speculation.") This shareholder-first approach to business ensures that your investments are not just speculation and will pay you like you deserve.

Obviously, these lists can be fertile ground for investors looking for stable income investment opportunities. In fact, some investors make an entire strategy just out of investing in Dividend Aristocrats. You can pick them individually, or if you prefer a more diversified, hands-off approach, there are several exchange traded funds (ETFs) that track both these groups.

These include **Vanguard Dividend Appreciation (NYSEARCA: VIG)**, which invests in 185 companies that have grown dividends annually for 10 years or more, and **ProShares S&P 500 Dividend Aristocrats (BATS: NOBL)**, which exclusively holds the stock of S&P 500 Dividend Aristocrats, each of which has raised dividends every year for at least 25 years or more.

These sorts of high-performing groups offer a valuable lesson for every income investor. No matter what sort of company you may be interested in investing in, a reliable record of dividend growth is a highly reliable means of pinpointing companies which have been there for investors in the past and will likely be there still in the years to come.

CHAPTER 15

PROTECTING YOUR WEALTH

While Doubling Your Income Along The Way

* * *

ALTHOUGH BONDS ARE OFTEN TOUTED AS A CONSERVATIVE, relatively risk-free income investment, they are still an investment — and all investments carry risk. When it comes to bonds, the main risk is the variability of interest rates, as set by the Federal Reserve, so in this chapter, we're going to explore a little-known investment called a Floating Rate Fund — which can protect your capital from the fluctuations in interest rates, *and* generate twice as much income as you would receive from buying standard bonds.

If you buy a bond at a particular interest rate and then interest rates go up, your bond is worth less (the return you will receive on that bond is pegged to the original interest rate, and no one is going to pay the same for your bond when they can buy it from someone else at the new, higher rate).

The following chart shows that bond values fall when interest rates rise. The line trending up in the chart shows interest rates rising from 0% to 2.25%. Meanwhile, the line trending down shows the price of U.S. Treasury bonds falling from nearly $113 to $105.

When interest rates rise, the yield on newly issued bonds also rises. As a result, the principal value of existing bonds will drop when interest rates rise.

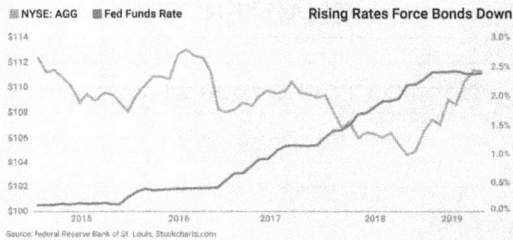

NYSE: AGG   Fed Funds Rate   Rising Rates Force Bonds Down

Source: Federal Reserve Bank of St. Louis, Stockcharts.com

This is the main concern in a rising interest rate environment. Let's say you've purchased a 10-year U.S. Treasury bond with a 2.25% yield. After buying the bond, the Federal Reserve raises rates by 0.25% That means newly issued bonds could yield 2.5%, instead of 2.25%.

Your loan doesn't get refinanced to account for that extra quarter point, so the loan becomes less attractive — the principal value of your loan on the market will go down, because there are now more attractive alternatives available for other investors.

If the Fed raises rates when you own bonds (meaning that you have loans out, awaiting repayment) then your principal value is worth less as a tradeable asset until that debt reaches maturity. So if you have a $1,000 bond out to a company, municipality or government, eventually you're going to be made whole and have that money repaid. But in the meantime — any time between now and the end of the bond's term, which could be many years away — the market is going to value that bond at less than par value because there are other options out there that were issued at a higher interest rate.

Historically, people have gotten around this by buying bonds with shorter duration, believing that interest rates are unlikely to change much in a short period of time. That may be the case, but it also means they receive lower rates, since short-term bonds pay less than long-term bonds.

Fortunately, floating rate funds can offset the uncertainty of fluctuating interest rates. Rather than owning bonds with fixed rates, these funds invest in bonds with variable rates, also known as 'floating' rates (some BDCs also issue debt on a floating rate basis, and some mutual funds also own floating rate debt).

Floating rates are tied to short-term interest rate benchmarks, such as the interest charged by banks when lending to other banks. This means that the funds' investments in the loans adjust quickly, preserving their value when other funds tied to fixed rate loans drop in value.

Fidelity Floating Rate (MUTF: FFRHX) is a good example here. Fidelity only owns floating rate loans — the debt they've issued to companies is structured so that if the Fed raises interest rates by that half point, the rate on all their loans goes up by a half point. They are not exposed to the risk of the Fed raising the rates and their loans getting left behind. Instead, the company receiving the loan pays the additional interest whenever the interest rate goes up. It's a great way to protect yourself in a rising interest rate environment.

Established in 2000, Fidelity has assets totaling almost $10.3 billion invested in 450 different holdings. Its portfolio consists primarily of bank loans, with a smaller component of corporate bonds, which is a mix that has paid off nicely. The fund's average annual return over the last 10 years was 4.3%. Meanwhile, the expense ratio was 0.7%. While 4.3%

isn't as big a return as some of the other investment classes we are discussing in this book, compare it to the standard, 'safe bet' investment of US Treasury bonds — at the time of writing, a 5-year Treasury bond was only returning 1.6%.

Since they are invested in bonds, the Fidelity fund is also well-suited to income investors looking to diversify beyond stocks, which is always wise for a balanced portfolio. And because the fund is designed to offset the risk of higher interest rates, FFRHX can be a good income investment during a period of rising interest rates.

To understand the risk exposure of floating rate funds, we need to understand a bit about credit ratings. Three agencies assign credit ratings: Moody's, Standard & Poors, and Fitch. Each of these agencies provide ratings to help investors determine the risk associated with various types of investments.

While they differ a little bit from each other, each system is based on single letter grades. For instance, Moody's might assign a company a AAA rating — the highest rating available, with the lowest associated risk. By contrast, a BAA is assigned to a company with less financial strength. Anything that's rated with a C is labelled 'junk,' which indicates the highest amount of risk. In the following table you can see the overall credit quality of the fund:

Credit Quality 5,7

AS OF 9/30/2019

BBB & Above

BB

B

CCC & Below

Not Rated/Not Available

Cash & Net Other Assets

Source: Fidelity Floating Rate Fund

Those ratings are key details companies have to disclose when they want to borrow money. A company with a high rating can get the most attractive terms, while companies with lower ratings have to settle for less appealing terms, such as higher interest rates. Fidelity specializes in issuing loans to companies with B and BB ratings — often the companies are in uncertain financial situations, negatively affecting their credit ratings. That lower credit rating boosts yields but, at the same time, can increase the chance of a default.

That's not to overplay the fund's volatility. The portion of the fund's BB-rated portfolio has historically delivered the highest returns, and only small portion of the fund's port-folio (roughly 6%) is rated B or lower. That's a very small allocation to loans with the greatest level of risk. They're mostly investing in well-known companies that just need an injection of capital, like Albertson's grocery stores, Bass Pro shops and Charter Communications. Following is a chart showing the fund's top 10 investments at the time of writing:

Top 10 Holdings AS OF 9/30/2019

12.63% of Total Portfolio

BASS PRO ESCROW TRM B 09/25/24
CHARTER COMM TERM B 4/30/25
CAESARS RESORT TRM B 1LN 12/24
INTELSAT TERM B-3 11/27/23
FRONTIER COM TRM B 1LN 6/15/24
MICRO FOCUS TERM B-3 06/21/24
FORMULA ONE TERM B NEW 2/01/24
ASURION TERM B2 2LN 08/24/25
LINEAGE LOGISTICS TERM B 02/25
GOLDEN NUGGET TERM B 1LN 10/23

447 holdings as of 9/30/2019 | 351 issuers as of 9/30/2019

Source: Fidelity Floating Rate Fund

And while some investors are not willing to deal with much risk at all, the difference in payout is significant. Compared with FFRHX's return (around 5%), a similar bond ETF — **Vanguard Total Bond Market (NASDAQ: BND)** — is currently paying a much more modest yield of 2.54%. This illustrates the disparity between fixed rate bonds and floating rate bonds — opting for conventional high quality bond funds may be safer, but it comes at the expense of investor payback.

Bonds have a place in a variety of income-generating portfolios. Funds such as FFRHX are more volatile, by design, and often offer superior returns, which allows investors to diversify into vehicles that can offer greater income without the interest rate risk that conventional bonds carry.

CHAPTER 16

AN INTRODUCTION TO OPTIONS

Double Your Income Events With This Powerful (But Misunderstood) Strategy

* * *

OPTIONS CAN BE A REMARKABLY REWARDING INCOME investment — as long as you do not misuse them as so many people have unfortunately done.

Many investors are intimidated by the idea of trading options, and have probably heard horror stories from people who have lost a fortune doing it. Options seem complicated, risky and time consuming. But that's a shame, because options can prove very valuable to investors looking to build an income stream. They're not as complicated as many investors assume, and they are not risky if you're using the right strategies.

Let's take a quick look at what options really are, and dispel some of that misunderstanding. Options are a form of derivative, which means its price is connected to (or derives from) the price of something else, such as the price of a stock or ETF. Options come in several forms and are a great way for income investors to make extra money from stocks they already own, or want to own.

People seeking safe and steady income should consider selling options contracts. If you sell a contract for a 'call' option, it gives the buyer the right to *buy* a stock from you at a particular price on a particular date. They pay you a fee when you sign the contract selling the call, and if they decide not to exercise their option on the agreed date, you keep your shares and the fee.

Selling a 'put' gives you the right to *sell* that stock to a buyer at a particular price on a particular date. You pay them a fee, and if you want to buy the share on the agreed date, you get it at a lower-than-market price. (You also have the option to do nothing and let the contract expire, although you will still be out the cost of buying the option.)

Many people prefer to take a chance and buy options contracts, because buying options contracts is incorrectly perceived to be an easy way to make bigger profits. If you buy a 'put' contract, you profit when a stock price falls. And when you buy a 'call' contract, you can make money when the stock price rises.

Selling 'puts' and 'calls' are some of the only options strategies approved for use in an IRA retirement account, and the fact that these strategies are allowed in those accounts is a signal that the government regulators do not see them as particularly risky. Their reputation for being risky is the result of people misusing these strategies and betting on the wrong types of stocks.

Trading options is a strategy best used on big and popular stocks and ETFs — on the 'headline stocks' of companies that you always see in the news. This strategy is not to be used on illiquid, small-cap stocks.

A WORD ABOUT OPTIONS

Some investors view options trading as a form of gambling — it's complicated and can be confusing. However, many others (myself included) believe that options, when used sensibly, can add significant muscle to any income investor's portfolio.

The issue is that a lot of investors don't apply common sense to options trading, and instead use options just to speculate. They think a stock's going to go from $50 a share to $60 a share and they want to leverage up in an attempt to make a killing. Most of the time, those investors will lose 80%-90% of their investment. But many of them are OK with that — they just want 1 out of 10 trades to hit a grand slam big enough to cover all their losses and then some.

But that's not investing. That's gambling. They're just hoping to pick the right one and make a killing, much like going to Las Vegas and playing roulette. That's not what I want you to do — it's way too risky when your income is on the line. The strategy we cover here is much less risky and is geared towards generating income in a predictable way. I look at options trading as a form of insurance, not speculation. If, for instance, you sell a covered call and the stock jumps in price, you can miss out on that appreciation. But the fact that you were paid a premium for the contract helps offset any money you may have missed out on otherwise.

Rather than treating options trading speculation, a random 'hit or miss' strategy, remember that every time you sell a call or put, you're going to receive a premium.

No matter the outcome of the contract, you're getting paid.

The reasons for investing in calls and puts are varied. For instance, if you expect a certain stock to rise in price, a call option gives you the right to purchase shares at a specified price at a later date, which allows you to pay less than what you would if you just bought the stock the conventional way.

Options are also an effective shield against market down-turns. By agreeing to sell a put at a particular price — lower than its current level — you can protect yourself from losses you would have incurred if you had just bought the stock and watched the price go down.

Each put or call contract represents 100 shares of stock. So, five contracts gives you control of 500 shares of stock. And this can be done at a fraction of the cost of simply buying the stock outright.

This means that buying a call contract typically costs 80% to 90% less than buying the same stock outright. Many speculators will therefore use options to leverage their capital and get more exposure to a trade. If the trade is successful, the profits can easily surpass 500% or even 1,000% gains. However, most of the time these contracts expire or are closed out at a loss before the expiration date.

Calls and puts can be an effective form of protection for both rising and falling prices — hence their general term 'covered calls,' which we will explore in the next section. But calls and puts can be difficult to manage (and if all this seems daunting, don't worry — I'm going to share some concrete examples in the next section).

Many investors want the additional income of an options investment without needing to put a lot of time and effort into managing it all, and prefer to combine this strategy with the more familiar model of an investment fund.

There are two closed-end funds that utilize this options income strategy.

One such fund is the **Guggenheim Enhanced Income fund (NYSE: GPM)**, which employs a hybrid approach — approximately 80% of its assets are invested in equities, including other funds. The fund augments those investments by using a careful strategy of selling call options (which carries the potential that the options will expire, rather than being called away, so that they can collect the premiums without losing the stock).

This multi-tiered strategy — earning income and gains through both dividends, and cash premiums received from selling options — has paid off. As of this writing, the fund's yield is 11.85%. It is an expensive fund to own (its expense ratio is 1.83%, which is much higher than more conventional funds). This reflects the high levels of activity within the fund, since more cost effective funds typically have lower portfolio turnover. And even with the high expense ratio, investors are still pocketing roughly 10% in yield, far surpassing the S&P 500 and other choices.

Another choice in this category is **Cohen & Steers Global Income Builder (NYSE: INB)**. Currently paying an 8.17% yield, INB invests in large cap common stocks, including giants like Apple and Sony. The fund also diversifies into American Depository Receipts (ADR), which are stocks that represent shares in foreign-based companies, and in other close-ended funds (which we'll explore in more detail later on).

INB also boosts income by using a covered call options strategy. That approach can help generate income during flat or down markets while offering additional protection when the market is rising quickly. INB also has a high expense ratio — 2.08% annually — but the substantial yield can still make this an attractive fund.

These funds will allow you to maximize your income using these options strategies. In my experience, using these strategies on specific stocks and ETFs is the best way to pull in an extra 18% to 30% in annual income. The numbers don't lie — selling options is a great conservative way to earn more income, and the following funds are an easy choice for people who want just want more income without all the work of buying and selling the options themselves.

CHAPTER 17

FAST TRACK YOUR INCOME WITH COVERED CALLS

This Options Strategy Can Increase Your Income Very Quickly

* * *

IF YOU WANT TO GET INCOME ROLLING IN AS FAST AS POSSIBLE, then this next section is an important strategy for you. While it takes some effort, this approach to increasing your income is highly effective — and ensures you get paid quickly.

Nearly every investor has shares of some stock in their account. However, most investors simply own the shares, wait for the stock price to rise, and collect quarterly checks from the stocks that pay them dividends. Unfortunately, they're leaving a lot of money on the table.

The average blue chip stock in the S&P 500 index is paying out a 1.9% dividend yield. Yet using a simple covered call options strategy, you could easily earn 3 to 5 times more income. That's the difference between earning 1.9% and pulling in up to 9.5% dividend. Plus, you'll still earn the regular 1.9% dividend. That means you could be earning over 11.4% income from the S&P 500 stocks you already own!

So how does this work? A covered call option gives the holder the right to buy a stock or an exchange traded fund (ETF) at a certain price (known as the strike price) by a certain date (known as the expiration.) An investor is effectively betting that a stock is going to increase in value, the hedge being that the investor wants to nab the stock at a bargain price.

The covered call strategy allows you to earn more income from your shares, by selling another investor the right to buy your shares at a future date at a future price you both agree on. Let's say I have 100 Microsoft shares, and right now they're trading at $135. I think that Microsoft is going to have a great quarter and their stock price is going to go up, and you think so too. We both want to make some money, so we sign an options contract where I sell you the right to buy my shares of Microsoft at $145 a share at any point in the next 3 months, regardless of how high the actual price goes.

In order to reward me for giving away the right to my shares, you pay me an upfront fee — you cut me a check, I get paid, and I've contractually agreed that if Microsoft shares go above $145, you can call away my stock at that price. For me, the risk is that if Microsoft goes to $160 and you call my shares away at $145, then I've left $15 per share on the table that I would have made otherwise.

However, I would still receive $10 in capital gains plus my premium for selling the calls, and statistically, there's a very small chance that Microsoft will go from $130 to $145 in 3 months, based on the historical data of share price volatility. So there's at least an 80% chance that you're going to pay me that upfront fee and walk away with nothing at the end of the 3 months. I keep the fee no matter the outcome of the contract, and the amount of that fee depends on the number of shares involved as well as how long I'm willing to allow you to exercise the call. Typically, the price is equal to 100 shares of the underlying stock.

The other risk is if Microsoft pushes below our purchase price minus the premium we sold. For instance, if I bought the stock for $135 and sold the premium for $5, the downside risk occurs if Microsoft falls below $130.

Because 3 months is a short timeframe, the downside is pretty limited — it's not like you're trying to predict where Microsoft will be in 3 years. Not a lot really changes at large companies in 3 months, since they're not very volatile. They generally stay in a stable price range and only gradually move up, so by using a covered call strategy, you can at least double the income you would see from the dividend, up to as much as 4 or 5 times that amount.

By doing this, you can earn the 1.3% dividend that Microsoft pays you for owning the stock, plus another 6% or so every year from selling the covered calls every 3 months. That means you can earn a 7% income yield instead of 1%.

If the stock continues to go up gradually, you make money by owning the stock as well — you get more income from the contract, plus the share price appreciation. And if it does happen that your stocks get called away, you get to keep the capital gains made on the stock and the total amount of call premium sold.

(There can be tax consequences to this, if you have capital gains on that stock. While there's a little bit more risk, you're going to pay taxes anyway, and this is a great strategy for people who want to earn more income and are willing to take a couple of extra steps. It's not great for someone who has owned a stock for 30 years and never wants to get rid of it, because there is a chance you won't have a choice about keeping it. But for people who are willing to lose a particular stock or are comfortable just replacing it, it's an easy way to earn more income.)

Selling calls works particularly well in markets we consider to be range-bound, meaning markets that are moving sideways. If we're in a bull market, and the stock market is going up 20% a year, this doesn't work well, because your stock will continue to be called away from you and you will miss out on the stock value appreciation. But it works great if stocks are moving sideways or if the stock market is falling — in that environment, your stock isn't going to be called away from you, and at least this way you're earning more income while the market declines.

Since we know that nobody is really successful at selling out during a downturn and buying when things are very low, this strategy allows you to hold all your positions and keep earning, to reduce your overall risk during the downturn and limit your losses. And if you continue to earn income, you might still end up positive.

Let's say the market goes down 10% in the next year. If you're using this covered call strategy with those Microsoft shares and you're earning 7%, then while the market goes down 10%, you're only down 3%. It's a way to reduce that downside in a meaningful way.

Covered calls are particularly suited to stable, blue-chip stocks. That's because they're less prone to any sort of significant movement up or down, lessening the chance that the investor who bought the covered call will actually execute it. These stocks are also more liquid, and have only a small difference between the bid and ask prices, which limits your downside risk.

Avoid covered calls with a really long duration — no more than 90 days or so. Although the premiums are lower on shorter strike timeframes, you reduce the risk of the investor actually executing the trade and taking your shares when you keep them short. And, if you do have to sell your shares, you'll need to buy new shares should you wish to maintain your position in the stock. It's best to buy them as close to your original price as possible, so often you will want to buy again right away.

When you take the time to dig in, covered calls are not as confusing or risky as people think. As I said earlier, covered calls and puts are the only two types of options that can be executed within retirement accounts — a solid sign that regulators don't view these strategies as reckless. They may be slightly more involved than simply buying or selling a stock, but the potential to increase your income make them worthy of consideration for any investor looking to get the most income from their portfolio.

DEEP DIVE: SELLING PUTS

Selling puts is essentially the opposite to selling calls. With puts, the seller is hoping that the stock price is going to drop. Selling a put option means that you can buy the agreed number of shares at the strike price prior to the expiration date. Selling a put positions you to buy the stock at a favorable price while, at the same time, earning a premium from the put contract. (Be careful not to confuse puts with limit orders. A limit order specifies a price you'd be willing to pay to buy a stock, but it doesn't carry any fees — it just lets you name an attractive price, with no payment for your risk.)

Let's say you want to buy that Microsoft stock, selling at $135 right now. You could go out and just buy the stock at $135, or you could sell a put: you make an offer that says you're willing to buy 100 shares of

Microsoft at $130 a share at any point in the next 3 months. So now you're on the other side of the transaction — you are paid a fee because you're willing to be a buyer at a price below the stock's price today.

If the Microsoft stock falls to that level in the next three months, you'll be able to buy those 100 shares at that price and essentially get the stock at a discount. It's good for you, because you accumulate more of the stock, and it's good for the seller, because they get a price that might be above what the stock has fallen to. Buying 100 shares of Microsoft stock outright would cost $13,500 — but you can sell a single put contract and immediately earn income. And you only have to come up with the cash to buy the 100 shares of stock if it gets "put to you."

If you want to use a covered call strategy on a stock that you don't yet own, you might as well start by selling the puts first, because once you get assigned the stock, then you can start using the covered calls. You might not get to buy the put for a few rounds, but every time you sell a put you earn income just like you do on a covered call — when you put that offer in, you're getting paid income for your offer. So you might get paid 4 times before you actually get the stock, and once you do get it, you can switch to covered calls until that stock gets called away from you, at which point you can start the cycle again.

Now, you should only do this with stocks that you do actually want to own. You don't want to get into these contracts unless it's a great stock that you'd like to own, because there's a 20-25% chance that you will actually end up with the stock. You want to be comfortable holding onto the stock, and to feel confident about the long-term prospects of the company. You should also feel comfortable at the prospect of selling calls on that stock for a year or two before it gets called away again.

This strategy basically lets you name the price at which you want to buy the stock. It's like if you walked into Walmart and saw some t-shirts you liked for $7, and telling an employee to call you when they've been marked down to $6 so you can buy them then.

This is an interesting way to name your price for any stock that you want to buy. It also means that you're getting paid income from stocks that you don't even own. When you're selling the put you don't own the stock, but you're able to collect income *because* you don't own it.

You can do this over and over, assuming that the stock price remains above your strike price. Of course, if you end up buying the shares at the strike price, you own the stock, which is what you wanted in the first place. This is why professionals prefer to sell puts. They know if done correctly, the strategy has the potential for them to acquire a stock for next to nothing.

But, to reiterate, when selling a put, you get paid to make a promise to buy a stock you want to own at the price you want to pay. Never sell puts on a stock that you didn't want to own at that strike price. That's how most people get in trouble, as they only pay attention to the income. They forget that they can — and eventually will — receive the shares.

In a sense, everyone stands to win with a put contract. For the buyer, puts can be an effective form of insurance. Should the price of the stock drop significantly — past the agreed upon sale point — the buyer can offload a certain number of shares at an attractive price, offsetting some of the losses from the falling stock price. The seller receives a premium at the outset of the contract, and is positioned to pick up a stock at a better price than it's at now. And if it never drops to that price point, the contract expires, with the premium in your pocket.

Like calls, puts are best used with stable, high-quality stocks that are not prone to excessive price movement. While a call is best used in a neutral market, selling puts is a bullish strategy. When you sell a call, you want the stock price to remain stable or decrease. When that happens, you collect the premium from selling the call — without being forced to purchase the shares of stock.

Both options offer an opportunity to boost the income potential with regard to stocks. Approach them as you would any other investment — prudently, with specific, focused goals in mind — to realize the most income potential with the least amount of risk.

CHAPTER 18

EARN $7,473 EVERY YEAR USING WARREN BUFFETT'S INCOME INVESTMENTS

Discover The Master Investor's Hand-Picked Stocks

* * *

L<small>IKE</small> I <small>SAID EARLIER IN THIS BOOK</small>, W<small>ARREN</small> B<small>UFFETT IS ONE</small> of the most successful investors in history,[1] and his company, Berkshire Hathaway, buys companies that are going to produce significant returns over the long term. Some of those stocks are income-producing, and in this chapter we're going to explore how you can create a portfolio with a selection of the stocks the world's best investor has pre-selected for you.

Buffett's approach to investing is to buy great companies at a fair price, and to invest in companies for the indefinite term. That's not to say that all his investments are held forever, but his approach is to look for companies that are going to stand the test of time — they're here today, they'll be here tomorrow, and in 20, 50, 100 years from now.

He tends to invest in things that are not fads, or popular right now — he wants things that will always be valued by the market. He likes big companies with strong track records, like Coca Cola, Geico and Kraft Heinz (Heinz has been making ketchup since the 1800s, and they're not stopping now).

Buffett is unique as an investment manager, in that he buys both publicly traded companies and privately held companies — he's willing to invest in anything, as long as it meets his criteria for financial health and good management.

The interesting thing about the Berkshire Hathaway model is that at its core, it's an insurance company. As a holding company, it now owns Geico outright, so all the millions of policies Geico sells are paid straight to Berkshire Hathaway. They own several other insurance companies too, which means that when all those companies write their insurance policies, Berkshire Hathaway collects the premiums, and those are used to pay future claims, but it also means they have a lot of cash on hand.

Most insurance companies just take that cash and put it in US treasuries, but Berkshire Hathaway invests it. And while most investment companies would borrow money and pay interest to make investments, because of its core insurance business, Berkshire Hathaway is being paid to invest.

Berkshire Hathaway has never paid dividends on its own stock. Buffett has said that he is going to do a better job investing the income from the stocks than shareholders, so instead of distributing those dividends, Berkshire Hathaway reinvests them in more new opportunities. Let's say you invest $100,000 in Berkshire and you want to earn 5% from it, his approach is that you should simply sell off the amount of stock necessary to generate the amount you want.

The average investor that thinks Buffett is a great investor and wants to invest with his company really has no option but to do this if they want to earn some income from their investments, but not everyone wants to sell off their stock every time they want some income. The next best thing, then, is to take Buffett's portfolio of stocks and simply purchase shares of the companies that do pay dividends.

Two-thirds of the companies in the Berkshire Hathaway portfolio of publicly traded companies do pay dividends, and by choosing these companies for your own portfolio, you get the stock-picking prowess of Buffett and the Berkshire team, along with all the income that those companies are paying (and this is where that $7,473 comes in, based upon a $10,000 investment in each of the 31 dividend stocks owned by Berkshire).

One of the most important things I've learned from Warren Buffett is that he believes that no one can predict where the stock market is going. He has often said that he doesn't think there's any way we can predict when a recession is going to happen, when stock prices are going to crash, or when they're going to soar. We're all guessing, so if we're right, it's because we're lucky. As a result of that, he's not focused on timing on the market at all — he believes that the best thing to do is to invest in companies you like, companies that are doing well and that you would like to own forever.

He advises choosing companies that will do well in good economic times and bad, because when the inevitable downturn in the economic cycle does eventually come, you want to own the companies that will continue to succeed.

The second thing is that Berkshire Hathaway always has a lot of cash on hand — to the tune of over $100 billion. They believe the best time to invest aggressively is when no one else will. Berkshire, by design, is positioned to be the lender or investor of choice at times when nobody else is writing checks. Back in 2011, Bank of America was in crisis after the financial meltdown — they couldn't issue debt, and they couldn't borrow money from anybody. The Federal government was stepping in to do its bailouts, and then Warren

Buffett and Berkshire invested in Bank of America. They put in $5 billion and got an amazing deal, because they were willing to write a check when no one else was. *The New York Times* reported that:

> "Under the terms of the deal, Berkshire will buy $5 billion of preferred stock that pay a 6 percent annual dividend, and receive warrants [a type of option] for 700 million shares that it can exercise over the next 10 years. Bank of America has the option to buy back the preferred shares at any time for a 5 percent premium."[2]

Every other big financial institution was sitting on the sidelines — they weren't making investments, they weren't writing checks because they were worried about what was going to happen in the future and wanted to hold onto their cash. Berkshire has specifically structured their business to take advantage of that hesitation, because it means they get really great terms on great companies. It's risky, but it often pays off, and the upside is extremely high.

In his annual letter to shareholders in 2016, Buffett said that the $5 billion of preferred stock paid a 6% annual dividend, meaning that Bank of America would pay Berkshire $300 million annually. In 2017, Berkshire also exercised their right to those warrants, buying 700 million shares to become Bank of America's biggest shareholder, which led to a $12 billion profit for Berkshire from this investment — an exceptional return by any standard.[3]

So not only have Berkshire and Buffett have become known as great dealmakers, but they are also fast to act. There are many stories of people who want to sell their company, and investment banks and private equity firms send in forensic accountants and spend months making a decision. But Buffett will have a phone call with them, look at the financials, and write a check in a week.

The original Bank of America deal was done in a *day*. And that's not because he's stupid or not doing his due diligence — it's because he knows what he's looking for and he's willing to act quickly to grasp an advantage. The Berkshire ethos is to pounce on opportunities when they're available, not getting caught up in the nitty-gritty and unnecessary details. When they see an opportunity to buy a great company at a fair price, they go all in.

A lot of people think of Buffett as being a 'deep value investor,' but that's not really the case — he doesn't want to buy crappy companies at a dirt-cheap price; he wants to buy great companies, at a fair price. This is a really important distinction — he's not willing to pay premium prices to get the fastest-growing stock on the market, but he's also not looking for crappy companies that are trading at cheap prices. He wants fair value in good companies at the right time.

Finally, his company firmly believes in the American dream. They believe that things are better now than they've ever been before, in terms of the standard of living, quality of life and economic prosperity. While the world may not be perfect today, it's better than it was 10, 20, or 50 years ago, and they believe that the outlook for capitalism and America is great. At every moment in history, there have been people who say that things aren't good, that we're going off the rails, the politicians are ruining everything, and that things are getting worse and worse. But if you look at the historical record since this American experiment started in 1776, things have continually gotten better. And if you had stopped and listened to the naysayers at any point, you would have gotten out of the market and stayed out, and you would have missed out on the greatest story of wealth creation in the world.

Knowing this, Buffett and his team choose not to worry about what's going to happen in the next year or two or five, because what's going to happen in the next 50 years is going to far surpass what happens in the short term.

They don't want to risk missing out on the long-term upside because they pulled money off the table and moved to the sidelines because of a short-term concern. Whether it's a worry about a particular president being in the White House, or because of a trade war with a foreign nation, or a conflict overseas, if we take money off the table at those times, we don't know when we'll be confident enough to get back in. That's how we miss out on the greatest wealth creation opportunities in the world — and investing with Berkshire Hathaway's strategies and companies is a great way to overcome that risk.

CHAPTER 19

COLLECT $1,120 EVERY 20 DAYS

One-Time Payments That Can Transform Your Wealth

* * *

WE'VE TALKED A LOT ABOUT DIVIDENDS, WHERE COMPANIES make regular cash payments to their shareholders, often around 2% each year. But there's another kind of payment companies make to their shareholders, and these one-time payments can provide income far beyond what's possible with many other investments. They're so powerful for building financial freedom that we've started referring to them as Liberty Checks. Whereas regular dividends usually pay out at a couple of percentage points, we've seen Liberty Checks as high as 20 and 30%.

Also known as Special Dividends, these payments are unpredictable, but they can provide a significant boost to your income if you know how to find them.

Usually a company will issue a press release to say they are distributing a special dividend to shareholders of record, and the reason for this is generally that something unusual has happened within the business. Maybe they sold off a division of the company and have a large cash windfall, or they've amassed a lot of profits they don't need for reinvestment — they're holding too much cash on their balance sheet, and wish to redistribute some of that money to the shareholders.

Microsoft did this some years ago — they issued a huge, multi-billion dollar special dividend. They had not paid any dividends for many years (although many companies who pay special dividends also pay regular dividends), so they had accumulated a lot of cash and they didn't need to keep it on-hand, so they returned it to the shareholders. Large companies who have been successful over a long period of time are usually the ones to pay Liberty Checks — companies like Costco and Ford Motor Company.

When any dividend is paid, the stock price is adjusted lower by the amount of the dividend. For example, let's say you have a stock that's trading at $100 a share, and the company issues a 1% dividend (either a regular dividend or a Liberty Check). Once that dividend is paid, the stock price will be adjusted down by that same percentage point — in this case, 1%. On a $100 stock, that's $1, so the stock price will be adjusted down to $99 when the stock starts trading again the day after the dividend is paid.

The interesting thing, though, is that when good companies pay special dividends for the right reasons, the share price will typically rebound (which is also usually the case for regular dividends, paid quarterly). When a company pays a quarterly dividend, for example, the stock will go down a little bit, but within a few weeks the stock is usually back up above where it was before that payment.

A lot of investors get hung up on this with special dividends and miss out on all the upside. If a company announces a 10% special dividend, investors focus on the fact that the stock price will be adjusted down by 10% after the payment is made. They forget to look at the income opportunity, or to take the long view that the stock will most likely recover to the same point or higher than it's at now, within 6 to 12 months of that distribution.

But unless you sell the stock after collecting that distribution, it really doesn't matter if it takes the stock a while to bounce back. If you buy something for $100 and it goes to $90, you haven't really lost anything until you sell the stock.

If you're willing to wait — because you think the company's decision to make that payment was a good one — then you will eventually be made whole by the recovery of the stock price, *and* you get paid up-front while you wait.

We've seen a big increase in these payments due to the Tax Cuts and Jobs Act that was passed in 2017. That bill said that profits from US corporations would be taxed whether or not they were held offshore or within the United States. For many years, companies would set up foreign subsidiaries and filter their profits through that foreign country to avoid paying taxes into their local economy.

A famous example of this is Apple. They sell products around the world, but all their European sales have been run through Ireland, because there's virtually no tax applied to the profit there. They license their technology to the Irish arm, so that even profits that were being generated within the US can be sent back to Apple Limited in Ireland, where they pay a total tax of 1% instead of 35%.

The interest rates in the wake of the 2008-2009 crisis were so low that this was an easy decision for corporations. If Apple (and many, many other companies like them), pre-2017, had $100 billion parked offshore, and they wanted to pay dividends, buy back stock, or build a $20 billion headquarters in Cupertino, California, they had two options: they could either bring the cash back to the US (and be slapped with a 35% corporate tax, and an additional 10% in California for a total of 45% tax), or they could go to any of the big banks of Wall Street, who would write 10-year bonds to be issued by Apple or the corporation in question, on which they would pay 3% interest.

There are news stories about this fairly often — a huge company with billions in profits is paying an effective tax rate of, say, 9%, despite being based in California where the tax rate is 35%. The reason they can do this is that they've gone to such great lengths to divert those profits to jurisdictions where there is little or no tax.

Once they've done that, though, the money is essentially stuck there. They can't bring it back into the United States (known as 'repatriation') without declaring it as income, so in the last 20 years or so, over $3 trillion in American money has been stashed away in offshore accounts to be out of reach of Uncle Sam.

To correct this, the Tax Cuts and Jobs Act said that retained foreign earnings would be subject to a one-time tax, whether or not the companies elect to bring it back to the United States or keep it offshore.

That means that if Apple has $100 billion parked in Ireland, the US government is going to levy a 10 to 12% tax on that money anyway. The government doesn't care if Apple keeps it in Ireland, or sends it to Luxembourg, or bring it back to the US; they're going to tax it either way.

Keeping that cash offshore withholds it from the American economy, and from shareholders, and that's why this change to the tax code is really important. It changes the dynamics within corporations, by encouraging them to not divert their companies offshore.

Some companies are still going to do it (there's still a big gap in what they would pay domestically and what they will pay in that one-time tax), but it certainly narrows the gap and limits the benefit the company receives from that strategy.

This is a major change in the landscape for big corporations, and it has meant that many of these companies are starting to repatriate their cash. They're bringing it back to the United States, because if they're going to pay tax anyway, they might as well have access to the cash to be able to make acquisitions, build infrastructure and create more jobs.

But for many companies, it doesn't make sense to build more locations, and there's only many raises and bonuses you're going to give employees. Instead, some companies do stock buy-backs, some increase their regular dividends, and some of them pay out Liberty Checks.

Ultimately, the cash these companies have accumulated doesn't belong to them: it belongs to the shareholders. Returning the capital to the shareholders is a very positive thing from an investor's standpoint, and the stocks tend to be rewarded with share price appreciation each time they do this.

Usually when companies decide to issue a special dividend, they put out a press release, so every time we see one of these press releases, my stock analyst, Steve, will analyze the company according to 7 key criteria related to the financial health of the company. This is because our belief is that companies issuing special dividends for the wrong reasons aren't good investments, even if you do get a payment upfront.

For example, a few years ago Nordstrom issued a special dividend, and we didn't think it was going to be a great opportunity. The reason they had so much cash is that they had sold off the division of their business that sold credit cards to consumers. For a lot of retailers, issuing credit cards and collecting the interest on those cards is a major cash flow business, and many retailers collect just as much revenue (if not more) from this as they do from operating retail stores.

So Nordstrom had sold off their credit card business and were using the proceeds to issue a special dividend. Our view on this was that the credit card operation had been really key to the company's long-term success, and without it, Nordstrom was no longer anywhere near as profitable or as financially healthy as it was previously.

In time, we were proven right — people collected the special dividend, but the stock price never recovered, and that's exactly the type of situation you want to avoid. Of course, it's nice to get paid a big chunk, but if you lose money on your principal investment, it's not worth it.

Other times companies who don't even have foreign-retained earnings will go ahead and take out a billion dollars in debt just to be able to pay a special dividend. This is *super* risky and is essentially mortgaging the future of the company, so that's another situation we want to avoid. For us, it's key to understand the fundamentals of the business. Whenever you're investing for income, it's all about the financial health of the business. You become a part owner in a business when you invest, whether you put in $500 or $5 million, and the financial health of the business is paramount if you want to get a worthwhile return on your investment.

So Steve has 7 points he looks for when he is determining whether he wants us to invest in a business when they announce a special dividend:

1. Pay-out of at least $400 (4% yield or $400 on a $10,000 investment)
2. Cash available to make the payment
3. Positive free cash flow
4. Financially sound capital structure
5. Insiders with "skin in the game"

6. Growing business and bright outlook
7. Paid from strength, not weakness

We like to invest when the payment is going to be a minimum of 4%, though the highest one we've collected was 41%. The company that issued the 41% dividend recovered its original share price within 9 months, which is a really great return, and it worked so well for them that they did it again a year later, issuing a 20% return and it recovered from that as well.

In an average month, we'll see 10 to 12 companies issue Liberty Checks of over 4%. Steve usually finds a couple each month that he thinks will be good trades (about 10% of the companies that are offering a payment of 4% or more). That means that for 90% of the announced special dividends, the financial health of the business isn't up to his criteria — the company's outlook isn't great, the sector they're in isn't performing, the management is doing something rash — for one reason or another they just doesn't pass our criteria.

Every morning and every afternoon, Steve looks through his alerts, reads each press release, and when he sees one that's over 4%, he starts doing the fundamental research on the company: what's their business, who are the executives, what's the financial performance for the past 3 years, what is does the future outlook, how does the balance sheet look, where's the money for the payment coming from and so on.

He does a deep dive on each of these questions, and we have a service called *Dividend Confidential* where we announce the companies that pass this evaluation.

Now, an individual investor can source the same information that Steve does each day. You set up Google News Alerts to search for these announcements, using a variety of keywords related to this — 'special dividends,' 'one-time payment' and so on. It just takes a lot of time.

We know most of our investors don't want to wake up every morning to read press releases and spend hours doing research, which is why you can just have Steve do it for you. He's already doing it anyway, and he is pretty quick at it. He knows within a couple of hours of reading a press release if a company is a good investment or not, and will usually issue an alert to our subscribers the same day a special dividend is announced.

The reason we're so quick to move on Liberty Checks is because timing is really important to maximize the amount you will earn — we don't want to wait 3 or 4 days to decide and give the market a chance to start moving up without us. Let's say the company is trading at $100 when they announce a 10% special dividend, and you have a month to buy stock to be included in the distribution.

Often, if the market views this announcement as good news, the stock price will increase between the announcement of the special dividend and the date it is paid. It might not move up the full 10% anticipated from the dividend, but it might go up by 5%. This doesn't happen overnight — it doesn't open 5% higher the day after the announcement — but it will happen over a couple of weeks.

So if you can move quickly after the announcement, you can buy the stock, see 5% in capital gains before even collecting the dividend, get the payment, and then when the stock is adjusted down 10%, your capital's value is already halfway back to where it started (because the stock price is adjusted down from $105, instead of $100).

On average, we're seeing a pretty high yield on these (often around 10 or 11%) and we're coming across new opportunities roughly every 20 days. Since Steve started delivering this strategy, the average company has made a 11.2% payment. This equals $1,120 for every $10,000 investment. For a lot of folks, this is a really great solution to being able to close the gap between their monthly income and their expenses, or to add a little extra cushion to their financial future.

Even if you only have $10,000 to invest in each trade, you can make $1,000 or $2,000 each time there's a special dividend announced. This is the type of high-yield trading used to be out of reach for folks who didn't have a million dollars to invest, but now that special dividends are being distributed so frequently, you can start earning more income quickly and regularly, with the added bonus of ending up with high-quality stock after the Liberty Check has been paid.

CHAPTER 20

THE GOLD IN ROYALTIES

Safe Income From The World's Original Investment

* * *

GOLD MIGHT SOUND LIKE AN OLD-FASHIONED INVESTMENT, but it's been around so long because it's just too good to ignore. In fact, it's the first investment people ever used to store and grow their wealth — choosing gold has been the go-to strategy of the wealthy for thousands of years.

Today, it's a powerful hedge against inflation, and can act as a safe haven for your money when the economic environment is volatile. And even though it's a finite commodity, you can also use gold to generate significant extra income if you invest the right way.

Now, you might be thinking, "Well, hang on! Mining for anything, even gold, is a risky business." And it's true — mining is expensive, time-consuming and unpredictable. Before you even start, you have to buy giant (and very pricey) pieces of heavy equipment, and you have to acquire the rights to do mining exploration in the area you're interested in. Once you've got all the paper and parts you need, you drill holes in the ground, look at samples of rock to see if there's any indication that the metal you're looking for is in the area you're drilling, and if it's not, you have to start all over again elsewhere.

This process takes many years, and millions of dollars. Any individual mining company might only have access to a few properties to explore and then mine, so their downside is very exposed (unless you're talking about one of the very large gold companies). As a result, the individual investor is also very exposed. But gold is a great asset to have as a source of security, and so the best alternative is to buy into companies that are known as royalty or streaming companies.

One of the first companies in the world to create the royalty streaming business model in this industry was Canada's **Franco-Nevada (NYSE: FNV)**. Founded in 1983 as a gold exploration company, Franco-Nevada purchased its first royalty interest in a Nevada-based gold mine owned by Western States Minerals. Before that deal, while royalty ownerships in oil and gas businesses were common, no public company had held a royalty interest in a precious metals mine. That meant the deal went on to produce a 1,200% return for Franco-Nevada and its investors.

Their whole model is different to that of the big mining companies, in that they don't own any gold mines outright. They have a team of just 29 employees at a corporate office in Toronto, and they're essentially a finance company that provides funding to gold companies. If a company has the right to exploration in a particular area, they're ready to start drilling, and need $20 million or $100 million, they often turn to companies like Franco-Nevada who will write a check and make an investment in the mine.

These investments could be debt or they could be equity; they often have a royalty component, meaning that 5 or 10%

of the gold that is taken from that mine goes back to Franco-Nevada (there are many royalty companies like this, but Franco-Nevada is the biggest).

For example, let's say Franco-Nevada lends a mining company $100 million at 8% interest, plus the company has to pay a 5% royalty on all the gold they find. From an investor's standpoint, this is interesting because you're able to make one investment in Franco-Nevada, and immediately you have exposure to lots of mines around the world. You diversify yourself just like you would with a mutual fund or an exchange traded fund, and it's a vehicle that's also designed to give you income, so there's a double upside. And to demonstrate just how powerful a strategy this can be, here's what an investment of just $1,000 has looked like over the past 10 years:

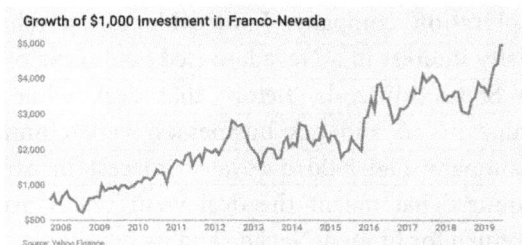

Growth of $1,000 Investment in Franco-Nevada

Source: Yahoo Finance

In the last decade, the Franco-Nevada stock has tripled in price. So while Franco-Nevada only pays out a small dividend, its recommendation in this book is based on their skill as great investors.

Now, gold is often seen as a safe investment in times of uncertainty, so when we're in late in the economic cycle, and we're starting to see signs of a downturn, we'll also start to see gold increase in price. It moves inversely with what's happening in the economy and with any worries about the US dollar. At the time of writing this book, we were late in an economic cycle, and gold royalty companies like Franco-Nevada were seeing better and better results as investors started looking for safe havens for their money. And it's not just gold — there are also silver royalty companies, and companies focused on other types of precious metals too.

To me, this is an interesting way to invest in gold and among the safest ways to do so. Most gold stocks don't pay a dividend — Franco-Nevada only pays a small one, but the real deal here is the combination of the dividend (returning some of the capital to the shareholders) with the capital appreciation of the principal investment. Franco-Nevada trades on the New York Stock Exchange, so it's very easy to buy, unlike various other methods of investing in gold. This year to date, 2019, the stock has gone from $70 a share to $84, which highlights the growth you might expect to see in your principal investment in gold royalties when the economy is more uncertain.

CHAPTER 21

TAKE FULL CONTROL OF YOUR MONEY: FIRE YOUR BANK

The New Accounts Transforming American Wealth

* * *

WE'RE IN A NEW AGE OF BANKING TODAY. GIVEN THAT MOST of us now pay our bills online, rarely (if ever) go to a branch office, and don't have a personal relationship with a banker at our bank — leveraging your bank for income is all about how much income you can earn in interest, and how much you can reduce the fees that we pay.

Back in the 1990s when I was starting my first online business, I needed to open a bank account. I remember going to First National Bank, a small community bank in my town, and my friend's mom, Barbara, was a banker there — she would help people with their mortgages, and help them set up accounts and get loans and so on.

I sat down with Barbara and she helped me open my checking account. Whenever I had an issue I would call her up, and she would sort it out. That kind of service and personal interaction was important and created a lot of loyalty, but that's not really the kind of relationship people have with their banks anymore.

Banking, like many other services, has become more and more commoditized as the Internet has transformed how we research and buy our products and services. Most people don't even have a contact for someone at the bank anymore. We have so much information available to us and so we're not stuck relying on one 'expert' who might not really have our best interests in mind.

This trend is only going to continue as older people become more comfortable with the Internet, and given that younger people are always going to be comfortable with online banking than going into a branch.

Online, we can instantly access the collective intelligence of everyone who has dealt with a particular bank: you can immediately find out what your options are and what kind of experience you are going to have. The banks no longer hold all the power in the interaction — the individual consumer is no longer at the mercy of the big institution, which gives us a lot more control.

Many people are still banking primarily with a local bank in the US, and that's not really necessary any more. There are banks now that don't have any physical properties, which allows them to give much more money back to customers. So if your bank is charging exorbitant fees, you can shop around now and actually do something about it.

In this section we're going to look at two different ways you can say goodbye to your big, expensive bank (that pays you almost nothing), take control of your money, and earn extra income while you do it.

EARN UP TO 12.4% INCOME BY CLOSING YOUR SAVINGS ACCOUNT

Most people save up their money by investing it in stock or by storing it at the bank. When you give money to the bank, it could be placed into a checking account, a savings account, a CD (certificate of deposit) account, or a money market account. And when you have money with a bank, in just about any type of account, the bank is then lending your money to other people.

If you have your money in a CD, for example, the bank pays you 1% interest per year, then turns around and lends your money to someone for their mortgage. That person is paying the bank 5% interest, so while it costs the bank 1% to get the money, they charge 5% when they lend it, and they earn the spread — those 4 percentage points in the middle. That's how the bank does business and how they make so much money every year.

But what if you could get rid of the bank-as-middleman, lend the money directly to other consumers of your choosing, and earn that extra interest yourself? While the risk is a bit more pronounced, you stand to make far more money on your savings than if you just leave it sitting in an account for the bank to cash in on.

This is where peer- to-peer lending comes in. With platforms like Prosper and Lending Tree, you're removing the bank, and instead, you get to choose the people or businesses you would like to loan money to directly. You earn the money directly, and there's a wide range of loans you can make.

You can base your choice on the credit-worthiness of the person borrowing the money — if you're making a car loan to a high net-worth individual, with a very high credit score, you might earn 4 or 5% on the loan (4 or 5 times higher than what you earned back with the bank).

But when you lend to someone who is less credit- worthy, the loan could have an 8, 10 or 12% yield on it. Obviously, a loan at 12% is going to be a lot more risky than a loan at 3%, so lender beware. But again, you will earn much more income on your money than just leaving it sitting in the bank. You can limit your downside risk by making small loans, but even those will add up to significant increases in your capital over time. And even if you choose the safe bets, the 3 or 4% you earn from those low-risk loans is much better than what you would otherwise earn from the bank.

Prosper, Lending Tree and Lending Club have all been around many years now, they're big companies, and you can choose loans that are FDIC insured if you want that extra level of confidence.

Borrowing from some current lending opportunities listed on these sites, you could earn 9.9% annual income on an $8,000 home improvement loan to a couple living in New Jersey. Meanwhile, a single man from Ohio is looking for an $8,000 debt consolidation loan — and he'll happily pay you 13.3% in annual income! These loans are highly rated and viewed as low-risk.

Meanwhile, there are plenty of opportunities if you don't mind the extra risk and are looking for higher yields. For example, a home owner in Indiana wants to borrow $9,000 to fund a kitchen remodel. And he's willing to pay 27% over the next 5 years to borrow the funds.

Another interesting option for peer-to-peer lending is the charitable micro-loan. Kiva is a platform with a 96% repayment rate, and it lets you lend to people in developing areas around the world who want to start or grow small businesses to support their families and communities. The yields on these are not as big as on some of the other sites, but this is a place where you can have a real impact on the world while also earning a decent return.

COLLECT 300% MORE INCOME FROM A FDIC-INSURED CHECKING ACCOUNT

If you like the idea of making more income from your savings, but want the security of a bank without the risk or effort of peer-to-peer lending, then a Kasasa checking account is for you.

Insured by the FDIC just like all the other big banks, Kasasa has been around since 2009, and it consistently pays out more income than any other account I've seen. It has all the things you would look for in a community bank, but it's very technology-focused and as a result, they're able to offer much bigger yields. Credit unions often give a lot of money back to their members and charge lower fees, but Kasasa is paying out around 4% interest. That's about 300% more interest than most other banks pay in interest, usually around 1%. Here's a quick comparison of the interest rates you will find at various banks around the country:

Column1	Checking Account Interest Rates
Kasasa	4.00%
BMO Harris Gank	2.35%
CIT Bank	2.30%
CapitalOne	2.00%
American Express	1.90%
Wells Fargo	0.05%
CitiBank	0.03%
BB&T	0.01%
Source: Bank websites.	

And if you're doing online banking, which most people are these days, it really doesn't matter if you don't have a direct relationship with the bank any more, or whether there's a branch in your town. What matters is how much you earn from that account, so if you can choose 4% over the 1%, why wouldn't you?

While most people aren't keeping tons of cash in their bank accounts, there are some obvious advantages to choosing a bank that pays out more.

Let's say you're saving cash to make a down-payment on a house. If you have $50,000 in the bank, because you don't want to have it anywhere there's any risk, the difference between 1% and 4% is huge — 1% is $500, but 4% is $2,000 — every extra $1,500 helps. It's not a life-changing amount, but it does add up. If you're going to have your money sitting in an account doing nothing, you might as well get paid more for it. These days banking really is a commodity, so the difference in choice comes down to how much you're going to earn from keeping your cash in your chosen account.

CHAPTER 22

COLLECT YOUR LEGAL MARIJUANA RENT CHECKS

Legalization Of Marijuana Is Going Mainstream

* * *

IN 2017, CANADA BECAME THE FIRST DEVELOPED-WORLD country to fully legalize cannabis. Meanwhile, the United States Federal Government has resisted tackling legalization.

Instead, the Federal Government has deferred to the 50 states and allowed them to set their own laws related to cannabis.

At the end of 2019, there are 33 states that have legalized cannabis for medical use. Plus, 11 states have approved recreational adult use of cannabis. This rapid geographic expansion is resulting in a migration of sales from the black market to legal markets. The following map shows the states in which cannabis is legal in one form or another:

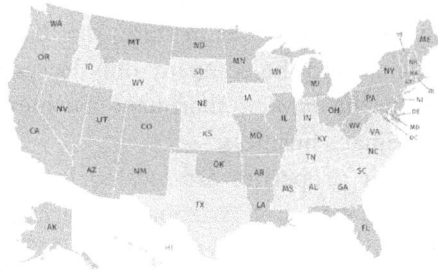

Source: http://www.drugpolicy.org/issues/medical-
marijuana

Current estimates suggest the black market is worth around $50 billion in annual sales. Meanwhile, legal cannabis sales hit $10.4 billion in 2019.

Current estimates suggest extremely rapid growth. Analysts at Cowen & Co. estimate that it'll become an $80 billion market by 2030. Meanwhile, Ackrell Capital expects the market to grow to $100 billion.

The marijuana business is booming. Yet most publicly traded cannabis stocks don't pay dividends. However, there's one exception.

Innovative Industrial Properties (NASDAQ: IIPR) is a Real Estate Investment Trust but unlike the other REITs we've covered in this book, Innovative Industrial isn't leasing hotel space or medical facilities. Instead, the company is focused on providing real estate for the medical cannabis industry.

Medical-use cannabis companies rent 42 properties from Innovative Industrial. In total, the company has 2.9 million square feet of rentable industrial space. Currently, the properties have a 100% occupancy rate.

The company has taken steps to ensure it isn't violating

any federal laws related to cannabis. That means Innovative Industrial only owns properties in states that have legalized medical marijuana. And the company only leases properties to companies in the *medical* marijuana business, not the recreational marijuana business.

Currently, their properties are located in several states across the country, including Arizona, California, Colorado, Illinois, Maryland, Massachusetts, Michigan, Minnesota, New York, Ohio and Pennsylvania.

In 2019, Innovative Properties was selected for the S&P 600 index. The decision to include the company in the index was a result of its size — and the fact that the company is operating within both state and federal laws.

This company is unlike other cannabis companies including **Canopy Growth (NYSE: CGC)**, **Cronos Group (NASDAQ: CRON)** and **Tilray (NASDAQ: TLRY)**, specifically because the company doesn't "touch the cannabis plant."

At the time of writing, Industrial Innovative is the *only* publicly traded cannabis REIT. And that has made shares of this stock a hot commodity. New companies focused on cannabis real estate have tried to go public, but have been unable to receive approval by securities regulators.

The stock has become a favorite for marijuana investors who want to earn income. Shares have jumped over 355% since an initial public offering in late 2017.

At the end of 2019, the company paid a healthy 3.8% dividend – paid out quarterly. That's approximately double the typical dividend paid from companies in the S&P 500 index.

It's the company's dividend growth that has investors clamoring to buy the stock. Two years ago, Industrial Innovative started paying a quarterly dividend of $0.15 per share. That's been increased by 420% — to a current $0.78 paid quarterly.

Innovative Industrial Properties offers the unique combination of rapid dividend growth and a high yield. That makes the stock an attractive way for income investors to bet on the explosive growth of legal cannabis in the U.S.

CHAPTER 23

HOW YOUR WEALTH CAN RISE WHEN THE MARKET DROPS

The Compound Power Of Dividend Reinvestment Programs
(DRIPs)

* * *

As has been mentioned many times throughout this book, dividends can be very powerful for investors seeking income. But dividends can prove particularly lucrative for investors who are willing to delay the pay-off, and that's where dividend reinvestment plans (DRIPs), also known as dividend multipliers, come into play.

Many investors just see a stock's dividends as a form of ongoing pay-out, and those folks with an income focus generally are very happy to pocket that cash and wait for the next pay-out. But if you don't need the income right now — maybe you're still working, or you have enough income to cover your regular expenses — you can opt into a DRIP to automatically reinvest those dividends to increase the amount of stock you own.

This has a few upsides (beyond making sure you don't

accidentally blow the cash when it hits your account). For one thing, it's an automatic investment strategy. Rather than manually choosing to continue buying shares in a particular company, DRIPs take the decision out of your hands, reinvesting those dividends automatically. This just happens over and over, which can add up a lot over time — let's say you made a $10,000 investment in a particular stock paying 3% in dividends, that's $300, which goes right back into your investment without your having to lift a finger.

Then compounding kicks in. Every time you receive a dividend, those funds are reinvested to buy more stock. That means you own more shares when the next quarterly dividend check is sent out. As a result, you benefit from the forced savings. And also from the fact that you continually increase the number of shares owned.

Let's say you buy 1,000 shares of a stock at $10 a share and select a dividend reinvestment program. The stock pays 3% annual dividends, with a yearly dividend growth rate of 2%, and the stock grows in value by an additional 2% every year.

Those are fairly modest numbers, but the results are impressive. After just 10 years, your original investment of $10,000 will be worth more than $168,000. By contrast, if you pocket the dividends every time they're paid, your original investment will only grow to $46,000.

DRIPs are also a good way to protect your investment against drops in stock prices. Although no investor wants to see a decrease, lower stock prices mean that your DRIP can purchase more shares at a lower cost. Sometimes the stock will rise, and the DRIP won't be able to buy as much with the dividend. Sometimes it's cheap, sometimes it's not, but you come out roughly in the middle with the added benefit of having all this happen automatically. This is called dollar-cost averaging, where you are continually accumulating shares on a regular, systematic basis.

This automatic progress is especially advantageous when the markets are dropping. When conditions are challenging, many investors just want to take the dividend and bail each time the payments are distributed. But your dividends are likely to be lower at these points, and you're not going to get a great price if you sell your stock, so having a DRIP in place can take the individual choice out of the equation here, allowing you to continue to build your holdings when bargain prices are often there for the taking.

But if you have to handle this voluntarily, making dozens of little decisions about whether to buy, sell or just hold, few investors can make it work. It takes a huge amount of confidence to accumulate shares when prices are dropping, even though that's the best time to buy.

DRIPs can also be an effective way to build portfolios with limited upfront cash. By buying the amount of stock you can afford and setting up a DRIP, you can slowly build up your holdings over time — again, with no effort required on your part.

But perhaps the most attractive feature of DRIPs from an income standpoint comes into play when the program has been running for a number of years. Since a DRIP investor has accumulated a large number of shares over time, the size of dividend payments has become much larger — just when an investor might decide to shift gears and begin accepting the dividend payout. The longer you wait to begin receiving payments, the larger the payment.

Lastly, setting up a DRIP program is a snap. When buying a stock, simply indicate whether you wish to receive dividend payouts or have them reinvested in the stock. In other words, set it and forget it.

There are, of course, a few other considerations to be

taken into account. For one thing, DRIPs are geared for investors with a long-range outlook. Reinvesting dividends is a great idea, but it requires a number of years for the full benefits to be realized — 5 to 10 years or more. That's because you truly need to have time on your side in order to benefit from the power of compound interest.

By contrast, a couple of years of reinvesting dividends is fine, but the resulting financial benefit is slight compared with a longer timeframe. This makes DRIPs an ideal choice for income investors who don't actually need the money immediately, opting instead to reinvest with the goal of larger payments later on. For instance, an investor in their 30s or 40s who doesn't need the additional income right away can build a substantial income stream that can be accessed when ongoing income can be more helpful, such as in retirement.

In conventional portfolios, dividends are also considered taxable income, even though an investor reinvests the dividends. But, in an IRA account, no taxes are due at the time of the dividend declaration — the investor can hold off paying those until they begin to withdraw money from the retirement account.

And, like other elements of income investing, it's never a good idea to invest in companies simply because they have a large dividend. Like any investment, look for a solid stock with reliable growth potentially, a reasonable price and, ideally, a dividend that has increased over time.

CHAPTER 24

THE BORING FUNDS BILLIONAIRES LOVE TO INVEST IN

Invest With The Best

* * *

HAVE YOU EVER HEARD OF CLOSED-END FUNDS (CEFs)? THE boring name seems to act like a disguise for a type of income investment that less than 3% of American investors actually own. Yet some of the best billionaire investors (including Warren Buffett, Carl Icahn, and Mario Gabelli) love to own these investments — because they pay.

With most investments, the current price represents a company's market value. Yet that isn't the case with closed-end funds. For all intents and purposes, closed-end funds trade like stocks, and most are listed on the New York Stock Exchange. Despite the diverse number of strategies, closed-end funds are far less popular than Exchange Traded Funds (ETFs) and mutual funds.

Just like mutual funds, closed-end funds can own any type of asset. This includes:

- Tax free municipal bonds US Treasuries
- Corporate bonds Dividend stocks Real estate Utilities
- Master limited partnerships
- Options strategies, including covered calls

There are 4 primary reasons that every income investor should load up on closed-end funds.

First, CEFs offer considerable liquidity. These investments trade during regular market hours — from 9.30am until 4pm Eastern Time. This is unlike mutual funds, which can only be bought or sold once per day. This means that you can buy and sell CEFs throughout the day, which is valuable during times of market volatility, when it can be beneficial to enter or exit a position during regular market hours.

Second, CEFs can use leverage to generate higher yields. Most mutual funds do not use leverage with their investments. However, leverage is quite common with CEFs. This means they can borrow money in order to increase the overall investment returns. CEFs are allowed to leverage up to 33.3% of the portfolio value, which means that many closed-end funds pay out yields that are higher than similar mutual funds or ETFs.

Third, CEFs have no investment minimum. Most mutual funds that have at least a $2,000 minimum investment — and some require a $5,000 or $10,000 investment. Meanwhile, an investor can purchase a single share of any CEF — often for under $20. This makes them more accessible to investors with less capital.

Fourth, CEF share prices can fluctuate compared with the value of the fund. Every day, shares trade on a public market and are quoted throughout the day. Meanwhile the fund publishes a daily metric called the Net Asset Value (NAV).

This measures the underlying value of the fund assets on a per-share basis.

This means it's easy to compare the current share price against the NAV. Shares can either trade on par with the NAV — meaning that the fund is getting the same value in the market as the value of the assets. Shares can occasionally trade at a premium to the NAV. And often, shares trade at a decent discount to the NAV.

CEF shares are attractive when the asset value is stable, and the share price is at a deep discount from the NAV figure. This means that the market may be incorrectly pricing the shares. And over the long-term, I'd expect the share price to revert in-line with the value of the underlying assets.

When it comes to CEFs, the winning formula is pretty simple. I like to find funds that offers a higher yield than comparable mutual funds and ETFs. And at the same time, I want to buy these funds at a discount to the value of their underlying assets.This makes it easy for you to make money in two ways:

1. Earn more income with every monthly or quarterly dividend payment.
2. Wait for the share price to rise, and achieve parity with the NAV of the fund's assets.

But what's particularly interesting about closed-end funds is how they're priced. Unlike most other investments, investors can buy shares of a closed-end fund at a discount

to market value. That's because the fund is affected by supply and demand. The fact that the number of shares is limited allows it to trade at prices above or below its real value. If you look at any well-known stock — say, Apple — all you see is the price. What you don't see is the actual *value* of the stock, which can differ quite a bit from the stated price.

In the case of a closed-end fund that invests in bonds, for instance, you can see the *value* of the bonds — say, $10. But the per-share price of the fund itself might be 90 cents. That's a 10% discount that an investor can nail down when buying into the fund—an immediate return. The discount further reduces risk. You're already ahead of the game because you buy your investments at less than market value.

Although closed-end funds can invest in all sorts of areas, the most common type of closed-end fund is municipal bond funds, which invest in bonds issued by state and local governments and agencies. Managers of these funds often seek to diversify broadly in order to minimize risk, but also often rely on leverage to maximize returns.

But there are also a few caveats to bear in mind when dealing with closed-end funds. For one thing, they require you to have a brokerage account to buy and sell your stock. Another key consideration before you buy is to understand that over half of these funds borrow money to invest. That can result in big returns but can also be risky. Share prices can fluctuate dramatically, resulting in unforeseen losses.

Additionally, be careful to examine the expenses of closed- end funds. Many closed-end funds have steep expense ratios — expenses that come out of investors' pockets.

Still, closed-end funds can produce terrific returns. One fund that we particularly like is **RiverNorth/DoubleLine Strategic Opportunity Fund (NYSE: OPP)**.

Opened in 2016, OPP is a small multi-sector fund, with less than $200 million in assets at the time of writing.

Like other closed-end funds, OPP shares are available at a discount to their net asset value. The discount is currently just shy of 6%. Additionally, fund management introduced a new distribution policy effective in 2019 — the fund will pay a distribution for the following year that yields a very high 12.5%. That payout is based on the average net asset value for the final 5 trading days of the prior year.

But, true to form, those advantages come with their share of potential downsides. For one thing, borrowing is substantial — some 26% of the fund's overall assets have been purchased with borrowed capital. Moreover, OPP's expense ratio — including the interest expenses for borrowing that money — is currently a hefty 2.67%.

Nonetheless, the fund's credentials are solid. For one thing, it's jointly managed by the closed-end fund specialist RiverNorth, and the well-known capital management firm, DoubleLine Capital. Management is effectively divvied up, with RiverNorth handling tactical income strategy and DoubleLine overseeing more aggressive income opportunities.

OPP is representative of the mix of risk and reward that characterize all closed-end funds — they're expensive to own and potentially volatile, but with pay-outs that far outpace other income investment options. For an investor willing to add a bit of risk to their portfolio, closed-end funds can be a lucrative addition.

CHAPTER 25

EARN 200% HIGHER YIELDS WITH PREFERRED STOCKS

Select Preferred Stock Designed To Mitigate The Effects Of Interest Rate Shifts

* * *

ISSUED LARGELY BY FINANCIAL FIRMS, TELECOM COMPANIES and utilities, preferred stocks have been around since the early 19th century. Something of a hybrid, preferred stocks are similar to bonds in that they're issued with a dividend coupon based on par (face) value. Preferred stock owners receive company dividends before 'common' stockholders, and should the worst happen and the issuing company collapse, preferred stock owners are paid before common stock investors from whatever remains are left to be paid out (after the IRS, of course, and other creditors).

For income investors, preferred stock can be a reliable and profitable addition to a portfolio, often yielding 6% up to as much as 25%.

Preferred stocks are highly structured in their dividend payouts, so investors know ahead of time just what they'll be getting. Like a bond, preferred stocks also tend to be sensitive to interest rates, falling in price when rates rise and vice versa. The price of preferred stock generally doesn't move much at all, so while common stock owners can profit substantially from a company's solid performance, preferred stock owners may see little, if any, change.

(So if you're considering buying preferred stock, just remember that you probably won't see any capital appreciation from your investment — just the dividends.)

For many investors, however, the yield of many preferred stocks almost makes price growth secondary. For instance, yield from the **Series A Preferred Stock from KKR and Co. (NASDAQ: KKR-PRA)**, a global investment firm, had moved past 6.5% at the time of writing. Another preferred issue — this one from banking concern **KeyCorp. (NYSE: KEY-J)** — also currently yields over 6%.

These yields are much better than what we see from conventional stocks, certificates of deposit and bonds, which often offer yields of 2% or even less. Preferred stock has another advantage beyond the yield — a verifiable rating. Like bonds, preferred stocks receive a credit rating from the major credit rating organizations, such as Standard & Poor's.

Ratings for preferred stock are generally slightly lower than the same company's bonds. That's because preferred dividends, like other forms of dividends, are issued at the direction of a company's board of directors. Should company performance lag, directors can choose to forgo dividends in favor of directing the cash elsewhere.

That leads to a couple of caveats. Many preferred stock issues are not cumulative, meaning that in the event of a missed payment, the company does not have to pay the balance of missed dividends to preferred shareholders before resuming payments of common dividends.

Still another issue is the possibility of stock buyback.

Most preferred stock is callable, meaning the company issuing the stock can buy them back from shareholders after a particular period of time. That doesn't mean that an issue will definitely be called, but it remains a possibility. If a preferred stock is trading above par value, investors can face a capital loss if their preferred stock is called back to the company.

Preferred stocks generally have short maturity dates, or no maturity date at all. That can make them vulnerable to interest rate movement, and issuers can often call preferred stock a mere 5 years or so after they're issued, further boosting the chances of capital losses for investors.

But there are types of preferred stock designed to mitigate the effects of interest rate shifts. Although many preferred stocks offer fixed rates, others offer adjustable rates, also known as "fixed to float" payments. That means the rate stays fixed for a set period — generally 10 years or less — then adjusts based on interest rate benchmark movement.

There are mutual funds and closed-end funds that have significant holdings in preferred stocks, which makes it very easy for the income investor to handle this more volatile asset. One such fund is **Nuveen Preferred & Income Securities Fund (NYSE: JPS)**, which allocates about 80% of its portfolio to preferred stocks and other income- generating securities.

Preferred stocks can be a good way to further diversify your own overall portfolio. Although their limited price movement potential may be discouraging to some, the fact that they're largely shielded from company performance can make them a suitable addition to a portfolio with lots of conventional stocks.

But like other investments, don't go chasing attractive yields blindly. Do some homework on the financial stability of the issuer, remembering that preferred stock dividends, like common stock dividends, can be suspended when a company falls on hard times, and the company is not required to repay the amount owing. Additionally, check the call date before investing — even the most enticing yield can be compromised by a relatively short call date, leaving you to reinvest your money at potentially lower rates.

Still, with attractive yields and low correlation to stocks given to greater price movement, preferred stocks are worth considering for income investors looking for a fresh avenue to boost their income streams.

CHAPTER 26

A GUARANTEED 9% INCOME FOR THE NEXT 25 YEARS

Get Paid By The Energy Revolution

* * *

As energy companies diversify, and the world gets bigger and more energy-hungry, we need to harness all our available energy sources like solar, wind, and biofuels — not only are these alternative sources good for the environment, they are great for your income.

Solar power is one of the most underutilized vehicles available to individual investors. And if you're starting to invest before you need the income, solar should be particularly high on your list of investments to consider.

I got a quote on a solar system recently, and discovered something that frankly shocked me. Basically, the system generates enough electricity so that I would pay back the cost (or break even) on the installation in about 9 years. After 9 years, I would have earned back my capital investment. Meanwhile, the system is guaranteed for 25 years, so after Year 9, I would essentially get free solar.

This means that the rate of return on the investment is around 9% — even assuming that I financed the entire system through a bank or credit union. This is a *huge* return. Where else can you get a 9% guaranteed rate of return over the next 25 years?

And on top of the spectacular returns, it's difficult to argue against solar power for many reasons. Obviously, it's a renewable energy source, and while it's great that it's environmentally friendly, it's also just there for the taking. It doesn't require millions of dollars and man-hours to harvest it, like we see with oil and gas, plus it's falling all over your house all the time and going to waste!

Solar power can be a great long-term investment — a form of income that, in large part, comes in the form of cost savings. Although its cost has come down quite a bit, solar power generally does require a significant upfront investment.

The average cost of a residential solar system in 2018 was $3.08 per watt for systems bought with cash (although you can obtain financing as well — solar loans are available with terms up to 25 years and adjustable interest rates) For a 6-kilowatt system (the average size of a residential solar system), that comes to $18,480.

But there are significant perks that cut into that expense considerably. First are federal and state incentives. Government incentives are changing constantly, but historically, the U.S. government has allowed a tax credit of up to 30% of the system's overall cost. Here's a breakdown from *Energy Sage* explaining this:

"The federal solar tax credit was originally established by the Energy Policy Act of 2005 and was set to expire at the end of 2007. A series of extensions pushed the expiration date back to the end of 2016, but experts believed that an additional 5-year extension would bring the solar industry to its full maturity. Thanks to the spending bill that Congress passed in late December 2015, the tax credit is now available to homeowners in some form through 2021. Here are the specifics:

- 2016 – 2019: The tax credit remains at 30% of the cost of the system. This means that in 2017, you can still get a major discounted price for your solar panel system.
- 2020: Owners of new residential and commercial solar can deduct 26% of the cost of the system from their taxes.
- 2021: Owners of new residential and commercial solar can deduct 22% of the cost of the system from their taxes.
- 2022 onwards: Owners of new commercial solar energy systems can deduct 10% of the cost of the system from their taxes. There is no federal credit for residential solar energy systems."[1]

You should also check with your state and local utility company about any additional financial incentives for solar installation and opportunities for selling the excess power you harvest back to the grid.[2]

Additionally, there's payback through much lower energy costs for your household. This will naturally vary from one location to the next but these savings can be significant and currently, the typical solar payback period in the U.S. is between 6 and 8 years — not a particularly long time, since anything you save (or earn through on-selling) is gravy.

A simple calculation lets you see what payback you might be looking at. For instance, if the cost of installing solar is $20,000 and the system saves $2,500 a year on energy bills, the payback period is 8 years. It's even more enticing when you look at that in terms of "internal rate of return," otherwise known as the expected rate of return that will be earned on a project or investment — roughly 12%. In fact, some estimates hold the average rate of return to be as high as 15%, particularly in states with high electricity rates. That rate of return may well increase in the future.

Although it's hard to anticipate whether solar installation costs will drop significantly, we're seeing predictable increases in the cost of buying electricity from power companies — we're all paying roughly 3.5% more every year for an essential service.

To take full advantage of solar, you can boost your returns with a couple of extra steps. For instance, some states and energy companies allow you to donate any "excess" power that you acquire to a non-profit or some other charitable organization. That's a tax write-off. And if you are generating more power from your solar panels than you're using in your home or business, many electric companies will apply a credit to your monthly bill (called "net metering").

You can also consider the increased value of your home if you ever decide to sell. For many home buyers, a house equipped with functioning solar panels can justify higher purchase prices.

There are, of course, a few limitations for solar power. Now, this isn't about the mistaken belief that certain parts of the country don't receive sufficient sunlight (here in the Northeast where I live, we get more sun than Germany, the world's leading adopter of solar power, and we have one of the lowest rates of received sunlight in the country). Rather, it's more about the specifics of your home and property.

Your roof's "azimuth" — the orientation relative to magnetic North — and its slope determine how much sunlight can be collected over the course of a year. A roof facing south will receive more sun than a roof facing any other direction. A flatter roof will generally produce more solar power than a steep one. Additionally, the roof on your home may simply not be big enough to accommodate a sufficient number of solar panels.

But, for many of us, solar power is yet another opportunity to generate income, boost the value of your property and, at the same time, feel great about doing what you can for a cleaner, more sustainable environment.

CHAPTER 27

THE FINE PRINT YOU MUST READ IF YOU WANT TO OWN RENTALS

How To Make Rental Properties More Lucrative

* * *

ALMOST EVERYONE WHO INVESTS WILL MISS OPPORTUNITIES every now and then — and I am no exception. Several years ago, a neighbor of mine in Vermont offered to sell me a townhouse located directly next to my office. His asking price was $217,000. As it happened, I had the cash on hand and could have paid for it free and clear. But I was focused on other things at the time, and I turned him down.

In hindsight, I missed out on a terrific income investment opportunity. Recently, I did some research on comparable properties and found that I could have rented the townhome for roughly $1,500 per month. After expenses, I'd have enjoyed rental income of about $15,000 per year — a tidy 7% return based on the asking price and more than three times that paid by S & P 500 stocks.

But, if nothing else, I got a valuable lesson out of the experience that I want to share with you — that investing in property that isn't your primary home can be a great way to generate income and accumulate a bit of a nest egg.

Now, being a landlord is not for everyone. Some folks are just not cut out for it. But if you're confident in your ability to manage and maintain rental properties, it can be a powerful addition to your income investment portfolio.

Most property buyers put 20% down as a deposit. In most markets, the resulting rent covers the mortgage, taxes and property maintenance, ideally with a little left over that you can pocket. But even if all you do is cover your monthly costs, you still have a 20% stake in the property with the remaining 80% being paid by someone else. Not a bad deal.

The next step involves some variables that depend on your personal circumstances. You can always take the conventional route of opting for a 30-year mortgage to finance the rental. On the other hand, if you're a little older than the average home-buyer — say, late 40s or early 50s — a 20-year mortgage can be more advantageous.

There are several upsides to a 20-year plan. For one thing, your interest rate will be lower than a 30-year loan (as of this writing, just under 4.5%, with slightly higher rates for a 30-year loan.) And if you pay according to the terms of the mortgage, you'll own the property outright 10 years earlier than you would on a 30-year loan.

Of course, your monthly mortgage payment will be slightly higher with a 20-year mortgage. For instance, with a $200,000 mortgage, you'll pay roughly $200 more per month with a 20-year than you will with a 30-year mortgage.

However, there's a wide array of choices at the end of the 20 years. On the one hand, since you now own the property free and clear, you have the option to continue collecting whatever you receive in rental payments. You can also choose to sell the property and pocket any appreciation the house has enjoyed over the past two decades. That can be a pretty substantial sum, which is why many people use this strategy — getting a 20-year mortgage in your 40s or 50s means that the contract closes out roughly around retirement age.

Appreciation depends on the dynamics of the local real estate market. While not every location is going to experience the same level of demand and growth, there are regions of the country that stand out when it comes to growing property values. Nor are they necessarily major metropolitan areas — for instance, Realtor.com's list of 2018's hottest real estate markets included big cities you would expect (like Boston and San Francisco) alongside smaller locations such as Racine (Wisconsin), Fort Wayne (Indiana) and Midland (Texas).

The type of property you choose to invest in can also play a role in the eventual payout. Multi-family locations are often the best bet, provided you can afford the deposit. Condominiums and townhomes are also attractive, particularly since homeowners associations' generally look after any property upkeep and maintenance — something that you as the landlord may have to take on should you buy a single family home.

Outside the consideration of finances, the level of involvement you're willing to have with a property is another major consideration. If you're handy and willing to show up at your rental with spanner in hand, then owning rental property may be right up your alley. If that thought makes you cringe, but you want rental income, it's best to choose low-commitment properties such as condos, or consider hiring a property manager to handle things. Just be aware that this can add to your total costs.

The idea of rental property can be appealing to investors who are willing to hold an asset for a long time and aren't worried about having to put some work into it. Not only can rentals provide a stream of income, their accrued value over time can offer a significant source of funds for investors looking to underwrite a comfortable retirement. That's putting an income investment to work for you in more ways than one.

CHAPTER 28

MY TOP PICKS: 10 STOCKS FOR THE NEXT 10 YEARS

The Stocks I'm Betting On For Excellent Income

* * *

HERE AT WYATT RESEARCH WE KNOW THAT THERE ARE SOME stocks that income investors should be paying serious attention to for the next 10 years. These stocks are great companies, that pay out strong dividends each year, and are set to grow into the future.

While it's hard to choose just 10, in this final chapter, I want to share a hand-picked selection with you from Steve Mauzy, who works with me here. Steve is a Chartered Financial Analyst (CFA) whose specialty is income investing. He particularly likes dividend stocks — they became the fashionable investment class since the 2009 recession, but dividend stocks have always been fashionable to Steve.

For the past 25 years, Steve has been advising investors on how to buy the right dividend stocks to collect immediate income and to build long-term wealth.

Not only that, but Steve has constructed a high-yield

portfolio of dividend growers, blue-chip dividend stocks, and tax-advantaged equity investments (including MLPs, REITs, and BDCs). His model portfolio provides investors with an average yield of 7.5% – far superior to yields offered by US Treasury securities and the S&P 500. Steve knows his way around income investing better than almost anyone in the business, and in this chapter he is pulling back the curtain on the 10 stocks he believes will generate excellent returns for income investors over the next 10 years.

TOP STOCK #1: APPLE (NASDAQ: AAPL)

There are not many companies in the world that have the kind of brand loyalty that Apple has created with its customers. People sleep outside overnight to be the first to get a new product, and rave about the genius of the technology. It's not surprising, then, that Apple is valued at over $309.5 billion, according to CNBC, making it one of the three most valuable companies in the world (along with Amazon and Google).

This enormous market cap is unlikely to go away any time soon. Not only does Apple enjoy that incredible customer loyalty, but they are also continuing to innovate, integrating 5G technology into their devices. Qualcomm predicts the value of goods and services enabled by 5G technology to reach $12.3 trillion in the next 15 years.

J.P Morgan predicts Apple will sell 195 million iPhones in 2020, up from an estimated 180 million in 2019, with 5G leading to a new cycle of iPhone sales on consumer upgrades. The total ecosystem for Apple's technology is massive — at the time of writing, there were over 1.4 billion active Apple devices in the world, of which 900 million are iPhones.

And Apple's upside is not limited to its hardware. It also

has a robust services business, including Apple Podcasts, Apple Music, the App Store, and iCloud. Several years ago, Apple's management set a goal to double the services business between the fiscal year 2016 and the fiscal year 2020. This implies over $48 billion of revenue in fiscal 2020 and a 19% compound annual growth rate from the fiscal 2016 base.

While that might sound like an outrageous goal, Apple is currently on track to exceed that target. In fact, the services businesses are so profitable that these revenue streams actually enable the company to continue developing its hardware: the gross profit margins on the collective services businesses are twice the margins of the product line — 63% compared to 31%.

Apple stock appears to be positioned well for long-term growth as a technology leader. Additionally, the company has a strong commitment to shareholders. This is evident by the continually growing dividend payments and aggressive stock repurchase program. With an ecosystem including the iPhone, iPad, iWatch, Mac, iTunes, Apple is creating a sticky audience of passionate and committed customers.

TOP STOCK #2: PAYCHEX (NASDAQ: PAYX)

If you've never heard of Paychex, don't worry. Some of the biggest companies in the world are not household names, but generate extraordinary amounts of revenue. Often, they do this by serving needs in the marketplace that just don't make the news, and Paychex is a perfect example of this.

They are the second-largest provider of payroll processing, human resources, and benefits services in the United States. Roughly 99% of Paychex's clients are businesses composed of fewer than 100 employees, with an average client size of approximately 16 employees. There are hundreds of thousands of businesses like this in the US, and they all need the services that Paychex provides.

As a result, Paychex has seen very consistent revenue and earnings growth: for the past 5 years, they have had 7.8% average revenue growth, an increase in earnings per share of 7.5% annually, as well as annual dividend growth of an average of 9.5%.

Paychex's high operating margins — 39% average over the past 5 years — ensures continued dividend growth into the future. The cash flow from their operations has doubled over the past 5 years, and there's a very strong trend in their free cash flow – $792 million in 2015, $1.19 billion over a trailing 12-month timeframe, which enables more share buybacks and greater annual dividend increases.

In mid-2019, the National Federation of Independent Businesses Small business announced that small business owners' expectations for sales, business conditions, and expansion are all on the rise, and the International Data Center expects this area to post a compound annual growth rate (CAGR) of 7%.

The market of HR Consulting Services is currently increasing at a CAGR of 9.7%, and for the more narrow US processing services market, IDC sees a CAGR of 4.5% between 2017 and 2022. But the biggest growth area of all is in the US market for business process outsourcing (BPO) services, where IDC expects a CAGR of 34.2% over the same time frame.

This is a huge amount of potential growth within the next few years, and a great opportunity for the income investor who doesn't mind holding 'secret stocks' like Paychex that aren't constantly in the news. It's especially promising when you consider that the company's dividend has grown at a 12.1% annual rate over the past 5 years (nearly doubling). Its share price has also doubled over the past 5 years.

And Paychex has one more trump card up their sleeve in the race for revenue: they completed the acquisition of Oasis in the third quarter of 2019, becoming the second- largest professional employer organization (PEO, companies that provide services to small and medium sized businesses) in the United States.

Paychex plans to offer additional insurance services to its Oasis client base. This should boost the company's revenues further in the near future, and so going forward, we expect Oasis to play a significant role in the company's overall growth, particularly its PEO business.

TOP STOCK #3: STAG INDUSTRIAL (NYSE: STAG)

Did you know that in 2019, e-commerce accounted for 10% of all US retail sales? And that this is projected to grow to 23% of all retail sales by 2025? This is exponential growth, as more and more people become comfortable with making all their purchases online. The e-commerce snowball is creating a whole range of logistical opportunities, one of which is the demand for warehouses to be distributed all throughout the country for fast shipping and smooth operations.

STAG Industrial is one of the companies that's thriving as a result of all this demand. An industrial real estate operating company, STAG acquires and operates single-tenant industrial properties throughout the United States. Like STORE, STAG is a REIT that has focused on a single industry. Where STORE has focused on serving the traditional retail market, STAG is looking ahead to the future and watching the growing opportunity of e-commerce.

Warehouses account for 83% of STAG Industrial's total number of properties, along with dozens of light manufacturing buildings, and warehouse occupancy rates are close to their peak levels. The pressure of the increasing demand for warehouse space is expected to accelerate supply, and STAG looks like it's going to step up and provide what the industry needs.

For every $1 billion increase in e-commerce sales, an estimated 1.25 million square feet of warehouse space is needed to meet all the additional storage and logistics of fulfilling those online orders. That is a massive growth opportunity, and it's going to pay off nicely for income investors who see the potential of this trend. And this is not just a flash-in-the-pan opportunity — industrial real estate in the US is a large, stable and developed market. There is an estimated trillion dollars worth of assets in the industry (half of which are these single-tenant industrial properties), and industrial real estate is consistently undervalued compared to other types of property.

So it's no surprise that STAG is a reliable monthly dividend payer. Their monthly dividend is increased every seven to eight months, and the stock currently yields 4.8%, which is significantly higher than the industrial REIT peer average. This is a great opportunity to add a steady stream of income to your portfolio.

TOP STOCK #4: UNITED PARCEL SERVICE (NYSE: UPS)

You're most likely familiar with UPS — it's the world's largest transportation company and whether you've noticed their brand or not, they've probably delivered to your very door.

Despite having to innovate quickly since Amazon burst onto the scene with their 1-2 day delivery choices, UPS is growing rapidly around the globe, also thanks to the wild growth of e-commerce. UPS is investing as fast as they can to keep up with their competition, having spent nearly $2 billion on its European infrastructure and $7 billion in the US in 2018 and 2019. The company did this by purchasing or renovating 22 new or renovated sorting facilities.

They are focusing extensively on international growth, having recently expanded to 14 new countries and increasing service to offer later pick-up times to 52,000 postal codes across Europe. Their standard delivery will reach more than 80% of Europe's population within 2 business days — a reach that even Amazon will have difficulty matching.

All this investment has been done very strategically; they're spending money to make money. UPS management expects a 35% efficiency gain, which will make for very attractive returns for investors. They have an expected earnings-per-share of 8%, and increasing domestic volumes of shipping suggest that this will continue to climb, paying out steady income to the savvy investor. Despite a bright outlook, shares have been trading at a cheap valuation.

TOP STOCK #5: ALTRIA GROUP (NYSE: MO)

Altria Group — formerly known as Phillip Morris — is one of America's biggest and most well-known tobacco companies with its Marlboro brand of cigarettes. More recently, the company has expanded with strategic investments in alcohol, marijuana, and vaping. The firm has a strong American heritage stretching back more than 180 years. Here's how they describe their company on their website:

"Our tobacco companies – which have been the undisputed market leaders in the U.S. tobacco industry for decades – include some of the most enduring names in American business: Philip Morris USA, the maker of Marlboro cigarettes, and U.S. Smokeless Tobacco Company, the maker of Copenhagen and Skoal. We also own John Middleton, manufacturer of Black & Mild cigars, and Nat Sherman, a super-premium cigarette and cigar business. And we have 35 percent ownership of JUUL Labs, Inc., the nation's leading e-vapor company. We complement our total tobacco platform with our ownership of Ste. Michelle Wine Estates, a collection of distinctive wine estates, and our significant equity investment in Anheuser-Busch InBev, the world's largest brewer. Our agreement to acquire a significant stake in Cronos Group, a leading global cannabinoid company, represents an exciting new global growth opportunity."[1]

While cigarette sales have been in decline for the past 25 years, the Marlboro brand still has a 45% market share of the tobacco market. Price increases have offset the decline in volume, and despite the slowdown, 38 million American adults still smoke daily. However, Altria has recognized that the industry is changing, and have proactively entered the smokeless tobacco market through the Copenhagen and Skoal brands. Revenue grows roughly 5% year over year in this market.

Not only that, but Altria is the front-runner in the e-cigarette market. It owns 35% of Juul Labs, the dominating brand in this new part of the industry. The global e- cigarette market size is projected to reach $47.1 billion by 2025, according to a new study by Grand View Research, Inc., which translates into a compound annual growth rate of nearly 24%.

The company is also diversified beyond tobacco products — it owns 10% of **Anheusuer-Busch InBev (NYSE: BUD)**, the world's largest beer brewer, and is poised to be a leader in the cannabis market thanks to its $1.8 billion stake in **Cronos Group (NASDAQ: CRON).**

Just as important as all these growth opportunities is the fact that Altria has an excellent management team. They are proven capital allocators who have led the company to deliver uninterrupted annual dividend growth for the past 49 years. That's a stunning record that is very appealing for income investors, and even more so when you factor in their dividend yield of 7.5%.

TOP STOCK #6: PEOPLE'S UNITED FINANCIAL (NASDAQ: PBCT)

People's United Financial, Inc. is a bank holding company that owns People's United Bank. The bank operates over 400 branches in the north-eastern part of the country. Its network of 422 branches in Connecticut, southeastern New York, Massachusetts, Vermont, Maine, and New Hampshire. And while it's a bold claim, I believe it is the best-run bank in the country.

In the past 10 years, People's United has acquired 9 financial institutions. The mix includes other banks, but also other financial businesses, including insurance and wealth management businesses. These acquisitions have helped People's United grow its basic banking business, and have also diversified its holdings.

One reason People's United is so good is their relentless focus on quality lending. The average FICO score on the retail (individual) loans is 763. A FICO score above 740 is rated "very good" at a minimum. This high standard is all the more impressive considering that People's United loan volume and net interest income (NII) have more than doubled over the past 10 years, growing from $16 million to $37 million.

This discipline also extends to its own investments. In 2009 People's United had $943 million in non-performing assets. By 2018, non-performing assets had been halved to $493 million. As a result, People's United is always ready to exploit acquisition opportunities when they arise.

Not only that, but they are also always ready to reward their shareholders. They've had 31 years of dividend growth (with growth even occurring during the 2008-2009 financial crisis), and today their dividend yields 4.3% — one of the highest in the banking sector. As far as the banking sector goes, this is one of my favorite stocks.

TOP STOCK #7: BOEING (NYSE: BA)

In the last 30 years, air travel has become incredibly popular, and far more affordable than anyone could have imagined at the birth of the industry. Fortunately for income investors, that trend doesn't look like it's going to change. In the decade up to 2030, Global Fleet & MRO Market Forecast are projecting a growth in demand for jets of 3.7% annually (to 37,978 jets).

While the 737 MAX debacle of 2019 was a tragedy, and should not have happened, Boeing has historically been a very strong company. Over the 10 years through 2018, sales increased at a compound annual growth rate (CAGR) of 4%. While this isn't very impressive, the company's bottom line performance is much better. Over the last decade, earnings per share grew 24% and dividend payouts increase at a 17% annual clip.

I believe it will continue to be a strong company: the MAX problem will be resolved, and earnings and revenue growth will return. And as you know, the moments when other people are hanging back are often the best moments to buy. The heightened uncertainty around Boeing today offers an opportunity to buy a good-quality stock on a pullback. At the time of writing, shares were trading well below the 52-week high.

And despite such a public failure, Boeing's projections for the future are bright. The 20-year forecast projects an average growth rate of 4.7% per year for passenger traffic and 4.2% for cargo traffic. They also project a $6.3 trillion market for approximately 42,700 new airplanes over the next 20 years. These are incredibly strong numbers, and since the dividend yield has grown steadily over the last decade, it's a smart move for income investors to get a piece of the air travel action.

TOP STOCK #8: CVS HEALTH (NYSE: CVS)

Healthcare is one of the biggest and most profitable industries in the entire country. We have an aging population, more wealth and more data than ever, and consumers are looking to apply that wealth and data to manage their health. CVS, which started as a regional chain in the northeast of the country, is now the largest retail pharmacy in the United States, holding 25% of the market share of this booming industry. It is also the leading pharmacy benefit management (PBM) company after purchasing Caremark in 2006. In 2006, Caremark generated $37 billion in revenue. In 2018, the CVS PBM segment (built on Caremark) generated $134 billion in revenue.

CVS also paid $78 billion to acquire Aetna, a leading diversified health care benefits company. The Aetna acquisition created a new business segment for CVS, health care benefits (HCB), and instantly added over $60 billion to CVS' annual revenue. The merger has tremendous upside potential for CVS, thanks to Aetna's rapidly-growing exposure to Medicare Advantage plans.

CVS also plans to turn its retail store footprints into "HealthHUBs," where customers can receive a variety of healthcare services. The HealthHUBs will contain Minute Clinics, wellness studios, dietitians, and even respiratory therapists. The roll-out of CVS' HealthHUBs in test markets has been highly successful according to CVS' management, and they are projecting a location count of 1,500 by the end of 2021. HealthHUB will increase CVS' market share even further, creating a surge in customer loyalty (and customer spending).

It's no surprise, then, that CVS bought a prodigious amount of its own stock in recent years. Between 2014 and 2017, the company spent between $4 billion and $5 billion annually buying back stock... and income investors should take note. CVS management knows they are sitting on a goldmine with all these deals and improvements.

CVS is a cash machine. The company typically generates around $10 billion in annual free cash flow. That compares quite favorably with the company's recent market capitalization of around $80 billion. With a growing 3% dividend yield, this makes CVS a long-term dividend stock to buy and hold.

TOP STOCK #9: ARES CAPITAL (NASDAQ: ARCC)

Ares Capital is the largest business development company (BDC) in the country, with around $14 billion in total assets and a $7.7 billion market cap.

As growth in the domestic economy continues, we are expecting to see ongoing demand for small business loans, and recent regulatory changes have made the conditions for such loans even more favorable.

In 2018, an amendment in the Investment Company Act of 1940 eased the leverage limits for such companies, allowing BDCs to increase their debt-to-equity leverage to 2:1 from 1:1 (subject to approval from their board and shareholders). This will help BDCs like Ares to reduce their portfolio risk by investing in higher capital structures — without foregoing the high rates of return they currently enjoy (and pass on to shareholders).

This change in the regulation is great news for Ares and the income investors who own this stock. With a high-quality portfolio of 345 portfolio companies with a focus on senior secured floating rate loans, Ares has provided a consistent dividend yield near 9%.

They have a strong history of dividend growth and supplemental dividends, and recently increased their quarterly dividend too. Ares is an income opportunity not to be missed.

TOP STOCK #10: W.P. CAREY (NYSE: WPC)

Like Paychex, W.P. Carey might not be a name you're familiar with, but make no mistake — this company is a hidden gem. WPC owns 1,168 properties, valued at $19 billion. Few REITs own more real estate, and while 95% occupancy is considered a good standard for a REIT, WPC's properties have an occupancy rate of 98.2%. That's virtually unrivalled, and this standard is representative of a company that's exceptional in every way.

Having amassed an extensive portfolio of real estate properties that it leases under triple-net terms, WPC's portfolio is diversified across property type: office (26% of rents), industrial (23%), warehouse (21%), retail (18%), with a range of properties making up the remaining 12%.There are very few REITs that are as balanced in property type as WPC, and their annualized base rent (ABR) is derived in similar proportions from industrial, warehouse, office, and retail properties.

International diversification is another yet benefit, since WPC takes its business across the Atlantic too. 35% of the company's ABR originates in Continental Europe and the United Kingdom. With such an incredibly strong presence in multiple markets and industries, W.P. Carey can opportunistically invest where it sees the most value in a way that less diversified REITs cannot.

As a result, W.P. Carey has continually increased its dividend over the past 21 years, and I'm not only talking about annual increases. Quarterly hikes have been the norm for the past decade. All that dividend growth is packaged in a yield — 5% — that few dividend growers can match. Adding this stock to your portfolio is both a wise move for diversification, but it also exposes you to a lot of income potential, thanks to their aggressive dividend growth and robust yield.

CHAPTER 29

THE FINAL WORD

THERE'S BEEN A HUGE AMOUNT OF INFORMATION TO TAKE IN throughout this book. You've learned a whole lot — you now know more about the economy, income investing and how to manage your money than most people in the country. Most importantly, you've learned what you need to do to take control of your financial future.

But there's one more thing you need to know.

The most important thing you can do now is to take action. You have all the information you need to start generating unlimited income for your future, right here in this book.

Too many people never start investing because they get caught up in never-ending research, always searching for one more piece of information that will make them feel ready. But the only way to feel ready is to make a start. That's not to say that you should rush into investments without vetting their credentials, but you now have all the knowledge you need to evaluate each vehicle and to move ahead.

Remember that you're not alone on this journey to financial freedom. Thousands of Americans just like you are diligently working to build up their income, taking control of their future and building up true independence for themselves and their families. This can take time, and it's important to take a long-term view. Sometimes it helps to be able to connect with other people who are on the same road, which is why I'd like to invite you to join our Unlimited Income Investors Facebook group — www.Facebook.com/groups/incomeinvestors/ — in this group you can share what's working for you, ask questions when you get stuck, and connect with other people who are exploring the same opportunities and challenges.

As I mentioned throughout the book, we've also developed several programs at Wyatt Investment Research that are designed to empower you to take advantage of specific investment vehicles.

One of the most popular is 'Dividend Confidential', a newsletter that shares our up-to-the-minute insights on Liberty Checks — the special dividend payments announced by big companies. 'High Yield Trader' is designed to help you increase the income you receive from the investments you already own, and 'Personal Wealth Advisor' gives you access to our entire team's research and investment strategies.

Now, if you need to generate a lot of cash quickly, these programs will not be right for you; they are specifically designed to build your wealth safely over time. But if you are ready to invest, and want more hands-on direction about where to direct your attention, then these programs can be powerful accelerants.

I hope this book has given you the confidence to pursue income investing as a wealth-building strategy. Remember that you have all the information you need to invest across all these vehicles, and that the most important thing you can do now is to take action.

Whether you have $5,000 to invest, or $50,000, you can

make a start today towards securing your financial future. It doesn't have to be complicated — the best strategy is the one you will stick to, so start with what comes easily to you. Take the parts of this book that appeal to you, and apply what works for your particular situation.

If you want support and extra insight, then join us in the Income Investors Facebook group, at www.facebook.com/groups.incomeinvestors/ and if you have any questions about those programs — or anything at all that you've read in this book — please reach out to me. My role is to serve you, to help you to work towards financial freedom, and to remind you one more time that unlimited income is yours for the taking.

RESOURCES FOR
EARNING MORE INCOME

Please enjoy these resources as next steps on your journey to earning more income.

The Unlimited Income Book Web Site:
www.DailyProfit.com/book

Listen to the Daily Profit Podcast:
https://dailyprofit.com/podcasts/

Join the Unlimited Income Investors Facebook Group:
https://www.facebook.com/groups/incomeinvestors/

Email Ian Wyatt:
book@dailyprofit.com

NOTES

1. AMERICA'S BEST INCOME INVESTMENTS REVEALED

1. https://www.federalreserve.gov/publications/
   2018-economic-well-being-of-us-households-in-
   2017-executive-summary.htm

2. USE 'INCOME INVESTING' FOR THE HIGHEST RETURNS

1. https://www.ft.com/content/2c910bce-7105-
   11e6-9ac1-1055824ca907
2. https://www.cnbc.com/2019/03/15/active-fund-
   managers-trail-the-sp-500-for-the-ninth-year-in-
   a-row-in-triumph-for-indexing.html
3. https://ycharts.com/companies/
   BRK.A/cash_on_hand

3. "WHERE DO THE RICH REALLY INVEST THEIR MONEY?"

1. https://www.linkedin.com/pulse/risks-rising-
   while-low-discounted-ray-dalio/

4. COLLECT 10X MORE INCOME FROM THESE SECRET "OFF WALL STREET" BANKS

1. http://www.arescapitalcorp.com/portfolio

5. LOOPHOLE CREATES VENTURE CAPITAL FIRM PAYING 9.9%

1. https://www.wsj.com/
   articles/SB100014240529702045737045771868 1
   3800414598
2. http://investor.htgc.com/Cache/1500123312.
   PDF?O=PDF&T=&Y=&D=&FID=
   1500123312&iid=4102290

8. HOW TO INVEST IN WARREN BUFFETT'S REIT OF CHOICE

1. https://www.reuters.com/article/us-usa-
   property-retail/us-retail-vacancy-rate-flat-at-102-
   percent-in-first-quarter-reis-idUSKCN1RE07D

10. COLLECTING CASH ON THE TOLL ROAD OF THE INTERNET

1. https://www.nasdaq.com/symbol/dlr/dividend-
   history

11. "HOW LONG ARE YOU STAYING?"

1. https://www.ustravel.org/system/files/

media_root/document/Research_Fact-
Sheet_Domestic-Travel.pdf

2. https://chathamlodgingtrust.gcs-web.com/news-
releases/news-release-details/chatham-lodging-
trust-announces-second-quarter-2019-results

12. INVESTMENT INCOME THAT'S 100% EXEMPT FROM FEDERAL INCOME TAXES

1. https://en.wikipedia.org/wiki/Lac-
M%C3%A9gantic_rail_disaster
2. https://www.reuters.com/article/us-energy-
transfer-permian-pipeline-idUSKCN1SF1N2

13. WANT BLUE CHIP STOCKS AT DISCOUNT PRICES?

1. http://www.dogsofthedow.com/dogyrs.htm

18. EARN $7,473 EVERY YEAR COPYING WARREN BUFFETT'S INCOME INVESTMENTS

1. https://awealthofcommonsense.com/2019/08/
who-has-the-most-impressive-investment-track-
record/
2. https://dealbook.nytimes.com/2011/08/25/
buffett-to-invest-5-billion-in-bank-of-america/
3. https://www.cnbc.com/2017/06/30/warren-
buffett-just-made-a-quick-12-billion-on-bank-of-
america.html

26. A GUARANTEED 9% INCOME FOR THE NEXT 25 YEARS

1. https://news.energysage.com/congress-extends-the-solar-tax-credit/
2. Check out the Database of State Incentives for Renewables and Efficiency's website for information on incentive programs for all 50 states: https://www.dsireusa.org/

28. MY TOP PICKS: 10 STOCKS FOR THE NEXT 10 YEARS

1. https://www.altria.com/about-altria/who-we-are

ACKNOWLEDGMENTS

I want to thank the many people who have influenced my life and made this book possible.

Thanks to my grandparents — Willis and Dorothy Cheney. A small gift of a few shares of Exxon stock sparked my interest in investing at an early age. Without this early experience, I may have never developed a lifelong passion for the stock market.

My parents — Bruce and Carol — were early supporters of my interest in investing. They allowed me to sell a few shares of Exxon so I could open up an account at Charles Schwab and begin trading stocks. They always supported my interested by buying me issues of *Barron's Magazine* and sticking *The Wall Street Journal's Guide to Investing* in my Christmas stocking at age 11.

My early passion for writing and publishing was cultivated by Raymond Schoenfeld at Beloit Memorial High School. As a journalism teacher and advisor at the high school newspaper called *The Increscent*, he helped me discover the value and importance of in-depth research and great reporting.

My family friends in the investment world also encouraged my passion. Special thanks to Bob Harrer who let me intern at Robert W. Baird during high school. And thanks to Andrew Davis for hosting me for a summer internship at his market making firm on the Chicago Stock Exchange.

Unlimited Income would not have been possible without the support of my colleagues at Wyatt Investment Research. Thanks to Laura Gale for collaborating in the development of this book. Also — to my colleagues Andy Crowder, Stephen Mauzy and Ben Shepherd for their assistance with research and analysis on a wide range of income investing topics.

I also want to thank my wife Carrie for her unrelenting support in writing this book. Thank you for supporting my passion and allowing me to put in long hours at night and on the weekends to get this important project completed.

Thanks to my children Macallister, Emmerson, Willoughby and Bellamy for being patient — even when I'm in the office working when you want to play.

Finally, I want to thank YOU. This book has only been possible due to your support. Successful investing — and earning more income — is of utmost importance as you prepare for retirement. And I hope that this book proves to be an invaluable resource that helps you live a wealthier life.

ABOUT THE AUTHOR

Ian Wyatt is the founder and Chief Investment Strategist of Wyatt Investment Research.

Since 2001, his company has helped over 3 million investors uncover huge wealth and income opportunities. And over 350,000 investors subscribe to his newsletters.

Ian's research has been featured in Barron's Magazine, Barrons.com, The Wall Street Journal's MarketWatch.com, Kiplinger's Personal Finance Magazine and Yahoo! Finance.

As a result of helping regular investors, Wyatt Investment Research has experienced tremendous growth of 1,303% in 3 years. The company was named #185 on the Inc. Magazine list of America's 500 fastest growing private companies.

In 2009, John Wiley & Sons published Ian's book *The Small-Cap Investor: Secrets to Winning Big with Small-Cap Stocks*. The book revealed Ian's successful strategies for finding small-cap stocks in the early stages of their growth trajectory.

Ian's newest book is *Unlimited Income*. Inside this book you'll discover how to build multiple streams of monthly income in order to secure your financial future.